Heroes, Rogues and Wisdom

A 20th-Century American Family History

Mike Miner

ISBN: 978-1-962402-41-5

Dedication

To my grandchildren
Giacomo, Lena, and Celia,
who all liked the fish stories best ...

Table of Contents

Family Tree

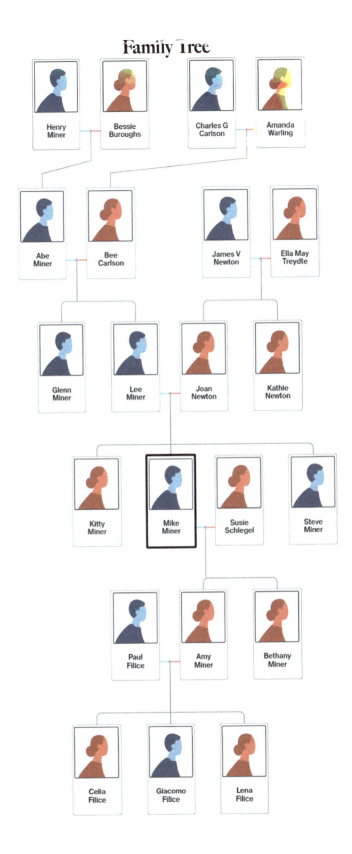

Introduction

S ome years ago—sitting alone in my favorite chair and reading a swashbuckling science fiction novel—I found myself suddenly yanked back into reality when the main character in the book offered this cynical counsel to a grieving friend:

> "Look," he reasoned, "You live; you die. Along the way you make some people happy, some others you piss off, and in a decade or so no one remembers you anyway."

It was such an appalling observation that I set the book aside to begin a long and, I'm afraid, completely unsatisfying conversation with myself, because no matter how I tried to refute the cynic's claim, there just wasn't anything wrong with his logic.

My grandfathers, I suddenly realized, were in real trouble.

You see, my grandfathers died when I was a very young man. They were both remarkable men, who had played huge roles in my early life, and in all the years since their passing I had consoled myself with the belief that they weren't really gone because they lived on in my memory. But, to the cynic's point, once I'm gone, and there's no one left to tell their stories, my grandfathers will vanish forever.

I suppose one could argue for a ripple effect, (i.e., their values will ripple down through generations to come), but there's no story in a ripple—no force, no personality, nothing that animates who they were. More importantly, knowing my grandfathers as I did, I can assure you that "ripples" weren't what these guys were striving for.

And the problem didn't end with my grandfathers. Yes, my grandmothers, parents, aunts, and uncles were well known to the generation following my own, but that only delayed the inevitable. All too soon the same cruel fate awaited each of them: *being forgotten.*

Ironically, all my immediate ancestors look ordinary at a glance or from a distance—made of the same sturdy stock that forms most of middle-class America—but up close that view quickly falls apart. Their personalities fly in every direction, and (for most) their abilities form a lopsided mix of great strengths and unholy weaknesses. As a group they may have been the most dissimilar collection of human beings ever assembled.

Yet, as different as they were individually, they had something extraordinary in common: their lives neatly bracketed the entirety of the 20th century. A period of unprecedented innovation, conflict, discovery, and change. A period when forces never before experienced moved them in directions no one could have foreseen—and they have the stories to prove it.

To be clear, I'm not suggesting that any of my ancestors achieved greatness (except, perhaps, for Bee). Indeed, some of them fell tragically short of ever reaching their life's potential. However, I can tell you with conviction, and not a little pride, that they all did something worthwhile, something worth knowing. What a shame it would be if all memory of them were lost amongst the countless and nameless multitudes of humankind who have lived and died in anonymity.

My intention, therefore, is to tell their stories with as much honesty as I am capable of bringing to the task, fully realizing that establishing the worth of another's existence is an occupation better left to the angels, and that only a fool would presume to be able to encompass the spirit and worth of a human life in a few words, no matter how carefully they are chosen.

I take my chance…

CHAPTER 1

Dawn of the 20th Century

For most anyone living in 21st century America, the early years of 1900 are likely to invoke an image not unlike the Dark Ages: a time when "life was nasty, brutish, and short." It's an easy impression to form and not altogether lacking in justification, when one considers that in 1900 horses provided most transportation, farming was still the number one occupation, and the average life expectancy was a mere 47 years (only a decade longer than their medieval ancestors).

Yet, as primitive as that long-ago time seems to us now, the people who actually ushered in the 20th century would have been astonished by that depiction. Propelled by the Industrial Revolution, they saw a country rushing into modernity. Railroads connected all 45 States[1] in the Union, steel ships crossed the oceans at will, and skyscrapers stood like monuments to progress in the great cities of New York, Chicago, San Francisco and more.

---

1 The territories of Oklahoma, New Mexico, and Arizona, wouldn't become States until 1912—Alaska and Hawaii not until 1959.

Flatiron Building, New York City, 1903.

It was a time when men like Andrew Carnegie and John D. Rockefeller amassed great fortunes and moved the Country in new directions, and when the *New York Times* confidently wrote in their December 31, 1899, issue, "We step upon the threshold of 1900 facing a still brighter dawn for human civilization."

Truly, this was no idle boast. In all of human history, no other country or people had ever looked upon a brighter future. Blessed with abundant resources, secure boarders, a common language and a shared heritage of Western European culture, America in 1900 was uniquely positioned for greatness.

From the modern observer's viewpoint, looking back at the 20th century is an exercise in astonishment—a period (as we shall see) when every single decade quite literally changed the course of history. But, of all the differences the modern observer would have noticed at the dawn of this new century, perhaps the most surprising would be just how rural the country was in 1900,[2] and it is here, in the heartland of America, that our story begins…

*   *   *   *

The place is Huron, South Dakota, a small midwestern town whose remoteness, even today, remains impressive. Surrounded by prairie, farmland and little else for hundreds of miles the vastness of the Northern Great Plains stretches out in every direction. Here the landscape east of the Missouri River (stretching from Iowa, through Nebraska, and across the Dakotas) is all but unchanging, and Huron's location is no exception—meaning the town's location is unremarkable in every measurable way. Indeed, Huron owes its existence entirely to happenstance.

In 1880 the rapidly expanding Chicago and North Western Railroad, needing a construction camp somewhere in southeastern

---

2   In 1900 the population of the U.S. stood at 76 million (vs 335 million today) and more than 60% of those Americans lived on the farm or at least in the countryside. Today, that number has shrunk to less than 20%.

South Dakota, chose the west bank of the James River. Gaining title to 800 acres of land, they named the new townsite after the Huron Indians—utterly clueless, it appears, that the local tribes were all Sioux, while the Hurons lived some 300 miles to the northeast in Canada.

Nevertheless, the name stuck, and Huron quickly became a jumping off point for homesteaders. In the years that followed, thousands of farm families began working the surrounding land and among them was a twenty-nine-year-old bachelor, who, in 1898, filed a claim on 160 acres just a few miles south of Huron. His name was Henry Miner— my great-grandfather.

Henry's parcel was located on the James River, and, to gain ownership under the Homestead Act, he had to accomplish three tasks: build a dwelling that measured at least 12 feet by 14 feet; cultivate at least 10 acres of land; and reside on the property for five years.

Relatively speaking, constructing the dwelling would have been easy. The walls were typically sod, windows were optional, and the roof a combination of wood beams, prairie grass and dirt. However, plowing virgin soil with a horse drawn plow, then planting and harvesting a 10-acre crop by hand, had to have been monumentally difficult. But as hard as producing a 10-acre crop must have been, one suspects the residency requirement—actually living in a 12-foot-by-14-foot sod house on the Great Plains—would have been worse.

Surrounded by his fellow homesteaders—each on 160 acres of land—it would have been uncommon for Henry to even see a neighbor in the distance let alone talk with one. There were blizzards in the winter, mosquitoes most of the rest of the year, and the ever-present threat of drought, prairie fire, and even the occasional swarm of locust.

Of course, conveniences like indoor plumbing, electric lights, and so on were missing, but what might have added most to Henry's frontier experience had to do with trees—or rather the lack of them.

Across the Northern Great Plains trees were all but nonexistent, which meant that fuel for cooking and heating was either twisted prairie grass or dried animal dung. Remarkably, the latter was preferred because it burned longer, although one wonders at the culinary dilemma this must have produced: would you like your homemade bread infused with the domesticated aroma of horse manure or the wild essence of buffalo chips?

Yet, as thoroughly unpleasant as the homestead experience could be, all across the American frontier people like Henry signed up by the thousands and eventually by the millions. In South Dakota alone homesteaders settled nearly a third of the entire state.[3]

For any resident of the 21st century, the popularity of homesteading is likely to be viewed with some skepticism (if not outright disbelief), until one remembers that neither Henry nor his fellow homesteaders were ever burdened with 21st century sensibilities. That said, speculating on what Henry thought was "normal" is surprisingly problematic, because in all of history no generation before his had ever been forced to redefine "normal" more frequently than Henry's.

---

3   The Homestead Act, first passed by Congress in 1863, underwent several revisions and eventually ended in 1986. During those 123 years nearly 4 million homestead claims were filed.

In defense of that bold assertion consider just two normal conditions that existed in the decade before Henry's birth in 1869 (and we're deliberately ignoring the Civil War 1861-1865): buffalo numbered in the tens of millions; and, settlers, bound for the West Coast, typically traveled by foot and covered wagon for six months to cross the western half of the U.S.

By the time Henry staked his homestead claim (1898) all the buffalo on the planet numbered less than 600 animals, and railroads could move passengers across the entire country—from New York to San Francisco—in just over 80 hours.

Typical homesteader sod house on the Great Plains, circa 1890.

Note: if that last bit about the railroad didn't produce an immediate OMG! response from the gentle reader, perhaps the following comparison will help place it into a proper "Aha!" perspective: If improvements to transportation had continued at a similar pace, today's traveler could circumnavigate the Earth in less than an hour, or by leaving early in the morning arrive in time for dinner ... on the Moon.

The buffalo (technically, "American bison") are a story in their own right. Extraordinary creatures in every aspect, they are born with an attitude that has doomed all attempts to domesticate them. Likely, this is due to a well-deserved self-confidence, because a full-grown male buffalo stands over 9 feet tall, weighs a ton (literally), and can run in excess of 35 mph. Most impressive of all (at 2,000 pounds) they can leap over a 6-foot-tall fence!

But as magnificent as buffalo remain, they were incompatible with farmers like Henry who could ill afford having wild herbivores eating their crops, and by the end of the 19th century buffalo were nearing extinction. No doubt this would have suited every farmer across the Great Plains, but, to the surprise of most, an unexpected movement developed to save them. Led by prominent figures like William "Buffalo Bill" Cody and future President Theodore Roosevelt (both former buffalo hunters), a captive breeding program was successfully established. Today buffalo number about 500,000 animals—mostly on ranches—with about 15,000 returned to the wild.[4]

Meanwhile, (and without any wild buffalo) Henry and his fellow Midwesterners forged ahead. Despite all the hardships they faced and the uncertain future that lay ahead, homesteading remained an unprecedented opportunity, and Henry, along with his neighbors and their big-city cousins continued to believe in "a still brighter dawn."

And besides, Henry seems to have had a plan…

---

4   Unfortunately, the buffalo represent a rare environmental success story. Worldwide the 20th century would witness the extinction of over 500 different animal species. The most famous example being the American Passenger Pigeon. In 1800 they numbered in the billions (with a 'B'), but were hunted to extinction for sport, food, and feathers. The last one in the wild was shot in 1902 and the last one in captivity died in 1914.

CHAPTER 2

Henry and Bessie

Two years after staking his claim Henry married Elizabeth "Bessie" May Burrows in 1900. She was 19; he was 31. Surprisingly beautiful, Bessie would have been a welcome addition to the Miner gene pool (which seemed to be heading in the wrong direction at this time considering how fearsome-looking most of Henry's five sisters appeared in the only surviving picture).

Diminutive even for the time, Bessie stood no more than 4 foot, 10 inches tall, but whatever she lacked in stature, she would prove to be every bit as tough as her fellow homesteaders. Delivering five healthy children (all of whom lived to into their 60s and 70s), Bessie herself lived to be 87 and survive her husband by nearly a quarter of a century.

How a nice girl from Minnesota (Bessie's birthplace) ended up marrying an "old guy" like Henry and moving into a sod house on the plains of South Dakota is unknown, but whatever her story one can only presume it contained seriously limited options. Regardless, the arrangement seems to have worked and in May of 1902 their first child was born, Alfred "Abe" Burrows Miner—my grandfather.

Bessie Miner, age 21.

While the majority of Abe's fellow South Dakotans were either immigrants from other States or from abroad, he could trace his South Dakota roots back two generations and his American roots back an amazing nine generations to 1629, when Thomas Miner left England and arrived in Connecticut.

Within that almost 300-year span there must have been some remarkable Miner ancestors. Sadly, all their stories have been lost, save one—Abe's grandfather—and, as it turns out, his exploits are completely worthy of our attention. So, for the next few paragraphs we will reverse our chronological direction and return briefly to the 19th century and the exploits of Nelson Preston Miner.

Though Nelson died years before Abe was born, he seems to have served as something of a role model for his son and grandson: both would become every bit the risk-taker and share the same aversion to occupational consistency.

Nelson was born in Ohio in 1824 and later moved to the Dakota Territories, where he married in 1849. Two years later he organized a company of 100 men, crossed the plains to California, and spent a year prospecting for gold. He returned east, started a law practice, became a justice of the peace, then entered the military. As a captain in the Dakota Territorial Militia, he helped suppress a Native American uprising in 1863 at the Battle of Whitestone Hill, and later served as a Union officer during the American Civil War.

Returning home in 1865, Nelson spent the next four years serving as registrar of the only land office in the Dakota Territory. He donated land and helped build the first permanent school in the territory. Then, in 1869, along with his brother, Ephraim, he was elected to the Territorial Legislature. Together, they served with enough distinction to get Miner County, South Dakota, named in their honor.

It was an impressive list of accomplishments, although, to be honest, the bit about "distinction" is somewhat speculative. The fact that Ephraim owned the local brothel and eventually died from syphilis does give one pause. Moreover, and with apologies to the good people of Miner County, having that particular piece of real estate named in your honor isn't nearly as impressive as it might sound. I know. I've been there, and Miner County might be the most featureless example of prairie land in the Midwest.

Remarkably, no Miners have ever actually lived in Miner County (Abe was born in nearby Beadle County). A perhaps boastful and unimportant detail; still, it does suggest a certain level of discernment within the Miner gene pool.

Or maybe not.

With regard to our ancestral namesake, the bar of discernment doesn't seem to have been set all that high, because South Dakotans in general don't live there either, and the few who do have been leaving at a rate so spectacular that the population has declined by nearly half in the last few decades.

Yet, whatever real or imagined shortcomings Ephraim and the surrounding countryside might have, there is to this day an impressive stone building in the county seat of Howard, South Dakota. Boldly inscribed atop the front entrance are the words *Miner County*—an enduring testament to those Miner Brothers from long ago, and a continuing source of some pride to the generations that followed.

Miners in front of Miner Courthouse, Howard, South Dakota 1997 (midway on Steve and family's move from Boston to Oregon). Left to right: Mike, Susie, Kitty, Matt, Jake, Steve, Dorothy, and Tom.

*   *   *   *

By 1909 Henry and Bessie had three healthy children and, with their family and farm both prospering, they were ready to put into place what was likely their strategy all along: selling the farm.

While most homesteaders became life-long farmers, nearly 40% sold their land and moved on to something else, and the Miner homestead—only a few miles from a major railroad terminal and straddling the James River—appears to have been more valuable than most.

The actual deal Henry put together to sell the family farm remains unknown, but it was enough to allow the young Miner Family some discretion in the next phase of their life, which (our narrator wishes to gratefully acknowledge) didn't include any part of the Great Plains.

Instead, Henry, Bessie and their three children (two more would follow in 1912 and 1915) moved as far from South Dakota as the railroad would take them, which at that time was Southern California.

For the Miner Family it must have felt like moving to another world, where Mother Nature, rather than actively trying to kill the lot of them with blizzards, tornadoes, locust, and the sheer boredom of endless prairie land, seemed to actually welcome their presence.

Here they found mountains, seashore, and abundant sunshine—all completely agreeable differences from their life on the Great Plains. But as pleasant as their new surroundings were, the real reason behind the move from South Dakota was the opportunity for Henry to shift from Old World agriculture to the new world of industry.

CHAPTER 3

The Aughts
(1900–1909)

As much as America had changed since Henry's birth in 1869, the first decade of the 20th century was to be absolutely transformative as industrial and economic forces catapulted both Henry and the Country in new directions.

Particularly for Henry and his generation, it must have been surreal. Still trying to wrap their heads around the end of the American Frontier and the triumph of the railroads, the dawn of the 20th century almost immediately confronted them with the automobile and the airplane (both in 1903).

This was also a time of Great Men—Thomas Edison, Henry Ford, Robert Peary, and the Wright Brothers to name a few. However, no one better exemplified (and shaped) this period than Theodore Roosevelt: president from 1901–1909.

Considered by most historians to be among the five best presidents in our nation's history, Roosevelt was as forceful, as driven, and as dynamic as the Country he led. On the home front, Roosevelt's belief in "a square deal for every man" saw him break up the railroad monopolies, reform banking practices, and institute the Pure Food and Drug Act. In foreign policy his slogan of "walk softly but carry a big stick" saw the U.S. begin construction of the Panama Canal in 1903 and to play increasingly important roles in global affairs.

He also famously met with John Muir (which led to Yosemite being added to the National Park system) and won the Nobel Peace Prize for his help in ending the Russo-Japanese War of 1904-1905. But, for all of Roosevelt's accomplishments and all the growing might of America, the best example of both must surely be "The Great White Fleet." (GWF)

Long an advocate of Naval power, Roosevelt sought to demonstrate to the nations of the world that America had become a global power, and in 1907 he dispatched 16 U.S. Naval battleships, along with various support vessels, to circumnavigate the globe.

The U.S. Battleship, Kansas, *sails ahead of* Vermont *as the fleet leaves Hampton Roads, Virginia, in 1907.*

Painted peacetime white, the fleet spent 14 months making goodwill stops in Japan, the Philippines, Australia, Egypt and more. At every port-of-call huge crowds swarmed the harbor to see the most powerful armada the world had ever known, and the GWF returned home to a hero's welcome in February 1908.[5]

But, as impressive as the GWF was (along with the advances in science and industry it represented) there was something else at work in the early part of the 20th century that would produce even greater and more far-reaching results: electricity.

This would have surprised nearly everyone at the time. Electricity was still in its infancy, and no one yet had a complete understanding of its properties or potential. Only large cities had been electrified— and even then, it was typically relegated to street lights and a few commercial buildings. Moreover, until the mid-1890s, Thomas Edison, America's "Greatest Inventor," was still vigorously promoting direct current (DC)—a dead-end technology that would have required dozens of power plants to electrify even a small city.

Nicholas Tesla solved the problem with alternating current (AC), which allowed large scale power plants (such as hydroelectric dams) to produce electricity economically and distribute it over vast distances. But soon electricity's mysteries deceived even Tesla's genius, who

---

5   While the GWF was an unqualified triumph on the world stage, the political skill Roosevelt employed behind the scenes was nearly as impressive. Unable to get Congress to appropriate funds for the GWF's circumnavigation, Roosevelt nevertheless ordered the Navy to proceed. Once all the ships were at sea, he informed Congress that, if they ever wanted to see the GWF again, they had to provide the necessary funds to bring the ships home. Completely outmaneuvered, Congress complied.

up until 1906 (and to his financial ruin) believed he could transmit electricity without wires.[6]

Nevertheless, the use of electricity continued to increase rapidly and when the Miner Family moved to Southern California in 1909, Henry became an electrician.

This is rather more impressive than one might guess. Astonishing, really, because electricity was all but non-existent in rural South Dakota—and wouldn't arrive to most of the state until after World War II—which can only mean that Henry's first day at his new job would have given real meaning to the term "no experience."

6   To his credit (and a fact most history books get wrong) Tesla's research in broadcasting electricity led to his accidental discovery of Radio in 1902, two years before Marconi.

CHAPTER 4

Southern California Circa 1910

T oday, if one happens to be among the 250,000 airline passengers who fly in and out of the Los Angeles area each day, it's impossible to look down at the megacity below and not to be impressed. The largest metropolitan region in the United States, its urban landscape seems to go on forever, and, to most of its 18-plus million inhabitants who are regularly stuck in traffic, it more or less does.

However, when Henry and family arrived in 1909 nearly everything outside of downtown Los Angeles was farmland and open space, and it was to the countryside—about 20 miles southeast of LA—that they took up residence.

Here, the foothills of the Santa Anna Mountains form the northern border of Orange County, and the Miners would have arrived to a backdrop of rolling hills, sagebrush, and, somewhat incongruently, hundreds of oil derricks scattered across the landscape.

The oil boom, which had begun in 1898 and would last until the 1940s, was in full swing and Henry likely went to work for the Union

Oil Company installing and repairing an ever-increasing number of electric pumps, motors and lamps.

In their new Southern California location, the Miner Family lived in what passed for a small town. Unfortunately, there's no reliable information regarding the local inhabitants at this time. Their ethnicity, education, social structure, etc., remain unknown. However, one can safely assume that as a group they didn't particularly value imagination, because in 1911, out of a population of some 500 residents, the best name they could come up with for their new City was "Tar." To be fair, they made it sound a little better by using the Spanish equivalent of "Brea" but still …

Regardless, the more interesting attribute of Brea and her citizens (along with Southern California in general) is that most of them shared a singularly strong connection: they were newcomers.

Brea oil fields, circa 1910. (Photo courtesy of the Brea Historical Society)

When the Miner Family arrived in 1909, only 38% of their fellow Californians were native born. Most, like themselves, had moved from other States, but fully a quarter of the population were immigrants. Indeed, whoever coined the term "melting pot" may have had Southern California in mind because in the 1910 census more than half the countries on the planet were represented, and it is to the immigrant experience that we turn to next.

CHAPTER 5

The Carlsons

Today and for decades past, immigration has been a divisive topic—and understandably so. The issues are complex, far reaching, and unevenly felt within society, but, regardless of one's position on immigration, the debate typically overlooks two fundamental facts: one obvious; the other not so much.

First, as even the most cursory demographic study will reveal, America *is* a land of immigrants and, unless you're among the 2% of the population that is Native American, no one need look very far in their family tree to find an ancestor who arrived from another country.[7]

Second—and this is surprisingly consequential—only a small minority of any population ever chooses to become immigrants. Even when faced with war, persecution, famine and more, most people stay put. To take just one (tragic) example, during Irish Potato Famine of

---

7   America has experienced three waves of immigration (beginning roughly in 1850, 1880, and 1960) and each wave of immigrants was followed by a backlash of anti-immigration sentiment—often violently expressed. Inconsistently—and this has been true throughout our history—the anti-immigrant faction has always held their own immigrant ancestors in high regard. It is only the current immigrants that are defective.

1845-1852, out of a population of seven million, only 10% emigrated. For those who remained, nearly 20% would die from starvation.

Among any given population, therefore, immigration has the curious effect of selecting the bold, the determined—the go-getters—and one of them lived just a few miles south of Henry Miner and family. His name was Charles "Gusty" Carlson (my immigrant great-grandfather).

Born in Sweden, he left home at age 19 to seek his fortune in the U.S. The year was 1884. Part of the second immigration wave (1880-1890), Gusty was among more than 5 million foreign nationals who arrived in America during that decade. Most were from southern and eastern Europe, but a disproportional number came from Sweden. In fact, as America found its population increasing by 10% during this period, Sweden experienced a similar population change but in exactly the opposite direction as one in ten Swedes left their country to come to America.

It must have been hard times and a hard choice, and though Gusty would have been surrounded by his fellow countrymen (and women), it had to be daunting to arrive in Stockholm from the countryside and climb aboard the steamship that would take him to the New World. Behind him lay everything he'd ever known; ahead was an unknown mix of risk and opportunity. It was a one-way trip and Gusty knew it.

He landed in New York City with just enough money for food and a train ticket to Chicago, where his brother had arranged a job in a meat processing plant.[8] Gusty didn't stay long. Whether it was an aversion to big-city life, a dislike for a job no one could love, or a longing to see the West Coast, within a few years he'd saved enough money to repay his brother and head to California.

Gusty likely arrived in Anaheim—it was the largest city in Orange County and had direct connections to the Continental Railroad system—but the real clue as to his whereabouts at this time was that, on July 27, 1890, he married Amanda Warling (a fellow Scandinavian immigrant) in that very city.

There are no family stories and little information about their early married life, but the couple eventually settled in the countryside north of Anaheim near what would later become the city of Placentia.[9] Here Gusty found employment with a large farming operation and eventually became foreman—a position he would retain for the rest of his life.

By 1904 the Carlsons had purchased a small farm of their own and had four healthy children—ages 4 through 12—when, on October 22 of that year, in what must have been the surprise of their lives, Amanda

---

8   Some 20 years later, the ill treatment and dangerous conditions Gusty and other immigrant laborers encountered in this very city and industry would be exposed in Upton Sinclair's book *The Jungle.*

9   The three adjoining cities in this portion of our story nicely reflect California's diversity: Anaheim is German for "home by the Santa Anna River," Brea is Spanish for "Tar," and Placentia is Latin for "pleasant place to live." *(BTW, apologies may be in order to those early residents of Brea. "Tar" might not be imaginative, but neither is it regularly mistaken for an organ that develops during pregnancy.)*

gave birth to twins: my grandmother, Bee, followed a few minutes later by her brother, Barney.[10]

Remarkably, Bee would live to see her 96th birthday, which means that the remainder of the 20th century unfolded right before her eyes. As a little girl living in the country, she'd taken her first airplane ride when a barnstormer landed his biplane in a nearby field. She watched her oldest brother go off to fight in France during World War I and watched again as her oldest son enlisted in the Navy during World War II. She lived through the Great Depression and the Great Society. She grew up when the "family car" was a horse and buggy and lived to see spacecraft exit the solar system. She saw Halley's Comet twice.

It was a life full of incredible experiences and, as a little boy, I well remember listening to her stories about growing up on the farm, which included horses, and cows, and outhouses, and all manner of hardships that were, apparently, normal in the "old days," but of all the farm-stories she told the most mindboggling by far was about being born.

Like their siblings, Bee and Barney were delivered at home, which, until the 1930s was the norm in the U.S. However, being twins, they were tiny, weighing only about four pounds each, and, as Bee would later describe, smaller than a loaf of bread.

As a little boy, Bee's "Birth Story" always made sense to me up to this point: being born, check; being small, check. It was the next step

---

10 Barney—a particularly easygoing individual—always joked that his twin sister, Bernice (Beanie when she was very little) had got all the nerves for both of them. She was always "busy as a bee." The name stuck, and Bernice became Bee somewhere in middle childhood. Apparently, it was a name she liked, because forever after it was the only one Bee ever used—even with her children and grandchildren.

I could never follow, because somebody put both those tiny babies in the oven!

Much later, I would understand. Keeping babies warm is critical and, lacking modern incubators, a slightly warm oven will serve the purpose. In fact, in the early 20th century this was normal procedure and done with practiced care by a midwife, but as a little boy all I heard was that my grandmother had been baked in a bread loaf pan.

Of course, Bee had other stories as well—a full lifetime of stories—and we'll get to some of them in later chapters. However, the "farm stories" were always her favorites, and in her later life, as she grew more forgetful, it was to these early memories that she returned to again and again. Eventually, I knew them all by heart. A few I heard so often I remember thinking (hoping, I'm now sorry to admit) they might wear out and disappear.

They never did, which turned out to be a wonderful thing, because Bee lived long enough to entertain (and inspire) a whole new generation of great-grandchildren, who were always properly astonished by the differences between growing up in the 1910s versus growing up in the 1980s-1990s.

There were stories about Bee borrowing her twin brother's pants when she was a little girl so she could wear them under her dress and hang upside down on the monkey bars at school; stories about the family's first telephone—a device that didn't arrive until Bee was a teenager and then used only for emergencies; the iceman making deliveries before refrigerators existed; and walking a mile down the dirt lane that led from her house to the main road, where she and Barney caught the bus for school.

There were scores more and if you listened long enough (and I did) there were themes that began to emerge. Bee's father and brothers, for example, were always cast in the starring roles. They built the bunkhouse, chopped the wood, repaired anything and everything, and went off to find jobs in agriculture and industry. By contrast, her mother and older sisters barely existed in Bee's childhood memories, and then only made cameo appearances in the kitchen.

It wasn't that Bee disliked the women in her family; she just didn't like the roles women were assigned in the early 20th century. Instead, she looked to the male members of her family for role models. They were the ones who did things, and from her earliest days she wanted to be like them—especially her father, who was always cast as the archetypal immigrant: honest, hardworking, resourceful, and successful.[11]

Another theme was the simplicity of farm life in the early 20th century. There were no rush-hour commutes, no cell phones screaming for attention, no emails waiting to be answered. Of course, "simple" doesn't mean "easy"—chopping wood for cooking, washing clothes in a bucket, and using an outhouse for a bathroom are all marvelously simple.

Finally, there was a thread running through all of Bee's farm stories completely at odds with the "Me First" mentality of today's 21st century. Yes, individuals still mattered in Bee's generation, but it was the family that assured survival, and everyone participated in that common cause.

---

11 He was also big. At over 6 feet tall (as were his three sons) Gusty Carlson would have towered over most men in 1910.

Not surprisingly, life on the family farm played a huge role in shaping the person Bee would become, and in two of her favorite stories (retold below) one can feel her core values taking form…

Bee's father remained the subject of many of her favorite stories. How he got up early every morning to start a fire in the wood-burning stove in order to make coffee before going to work—a tradition Bee would maintain (on a gas stove) for as long as I knew her; his constant work improving the family farm, and the story she told most often, his attention to a kerosene lamp

Before she ever started her formal education, Bee showed promise as a student, and her father was quick to recognize his youngest daughter's potential. Apparently, Gusty provided some early assistance with math, but his real contribution to Bee's education was the encouragement and support he put into action.

Electricity as a source of energy and light for homes was virtually unknown before Bee was born, and it didn't arrive on the farm until she was in high school. Up until then, when the sun went down, kerosene lamps provided all light inside their house. Versions of these lamps had been used for centuries, and upon entering school, Bee was given one of her very own, which allowed her to complete her homework at night.

While these lamps actually worked quite well, they did require regular maintenance and it soon became her father's self-assigned task to care for that particular lamp. He refilled the kerosene, trimmed the wick as necessary, and washed the glass chimney every day so that each night his youngest daughter had all the light she needed to study by.

For Bee, everything good and wonderful about her father seemed to be wrapped up in that simple act, and every time she watched him clean that chimney (and every time she re-told this story), I think she heard him say, "I love you."

*   *   *   *

The Carlson family farm included a modest home, a barn, and later a tank house (completed in 1912, it provided running water for the first time). It also included an orange grove, which produced a cash crop each year and provided most of the family's disposable income. Every orange tree was therefore treated with the care and respect it deserved. In Southern California this especially meant regular irrigation, and when Bee and Barney were only 5 years old, they began helping with this important task.

Irrigating an orange grove in the 1910s was a scene right out of ancient Egypt. After paying a fee to the local water company, one to three boards would be removed from a short section of the nearby canal, which allowed water to spill into the ditch leading to their property. By carefully directing the water over a specific number of hours, the entire orchard would be flooded. It became the twins' job to keep that irrigation ditch clean and free of debris so that their father actually got all the water he had paid for.

The job took hours, and one can easily imagine the drudgery of waiting by that ditch watching an endless stream of water go by, but Bee didn't remember it that way. Together with Barney they would walk along the ditch, and, while keeping a close eye out for leaks or clogs, they invented games: sticks would become great ocean liners, and floating leaves were targets for well-aimed rocks. In Bee's memory, watching that ditch with her twin brother was the best job she ever had.

*   *   *   *

A MINER SIDE NOTE

WATERWORKS

Just over 100 years after the irrigation story above—in a circle-of-life episode that would have made little Beanie (Bee) Carlson giggle with delight—her great-great-granddaughters Lena and Celia, would be found similarly engaged. Like Bee, Lena and Celia (then ages 5 and 3½) lived on a small farm at the end of a dirt road and, though their family didn't have an orange grove, they did have an unusually large garden.

Here (with the added help of a garden hose and a few short pieces of PVC pipe) the girls and I spent part of a summer afternoon building dams, canals, and aqueducts that cris-crossed the garden and ran down an adjoining slope.

True, our waterworks didn't possess the importance of Bee and Barnie's irrigation ditch, but, judging by how muddy Lena and Celia both were by the end of our project, they enjoyed the process every bit as much as their great-great-grandmother had a century before.

Of course, not every job on the farm was an adventure. Most of the stories Bee told—milking the cow, washing clothes by hand, or hand pumping every gallon of water the family used—sounded tedious at best, while others, like sharing a single outhouse with seven other family members, were just plain awful.

In my own childhood, when I first began hearing some of Bee's farm stories, I was fascinated. The hardship they represented was incredible, but mostly, I was awestruck by how nonchalant she was about all of it. When I once asked how she could have possibly emptied a chamber pot, Bee's simple response was, "Well, it wasn't going to empty itself."

That comment was classic Bee. She grew up at a time and place where work (and it was often hard physical work) was inseparably linked to living, and that connection remained at the core of her being. For Bee work was a lot like breathing; it was something you just did.

CHAPTER 6

A Tumultuous Decade

Throughout the 1910s, while the Miners and Carlsons (with 11 children between them) were absorbed in the everyday challenges of family life, the rest of the world spent that decade lurching from one catastrophe to the next.

Across the globe revolutions would convulse Mexico, then spread to much of Europe, all of China, and culminate in the Russian Revolution of 1917, which all by itself would kill 10-million (mostly peasant) Russian citizens. Much worse, from 1914-1918—in what was arguably the most senseless conflict in human history— World War I slaughtered 20-million people. Finally, as though participating in some kind of demonic competition, the Spanish Flu arrived in 1918 and killed an estimated 50 million people worldwide before mysteriously disappearing two years later.

Yet, through all the carnage of the 1910s humankind continued its rush towards modernity, and nowhere was this more apparent and more economically successful than in California. From just under 1.5 million people in 1900, the state's population would double by 1920 and double again before 1940. By 1960 California would become the most populous state in the Nation and in the 1980s would surpass the entire population of Canada—a country almost 25 times larger!

Much of this achievement comes down to simple geography—California is blessed with natural resources like nowhere else on earth. The Central Valley, for example, is so astonishingly fertile that, while making up just 1% of total U.S. agricultural land, provides more than half the nation's fruits and vegetables and a quarter of all other food production. Across the rest of the state are millions of acres of forest, vast mineral deposits, and the priceless benefit of multiple natural harbors along nearly 1,000 miles of coastline.

But, resources alone don't build civilizations. It takes people, talent, and vision, and California was blessed with those as well. Including (and this is particularly surprising given today's fraught political climate) a state government that got things done.

In 1910, with $18 million dollars in bond money, the state began construction of its first highway system. Promising to build 3,100 miles of new highway, link every county seat, and reach from Mexico to the Oregon border, the project quickly proved to be as long on vision as it was short on fiscal responsibility—meaning it ran out of money almost immediately.

Undeterred—and in a pattern familiar to taxpayers everywhere—additional bonds were approved, and the project eventually completed for an additional $35 million dollars. Still, it remains an impressive achievement. 3,100 miles of highway is more than enough to cross the entire Continental United States. Moreover, if done today (and this assumes a continuous string of victories, against a continuous string of lawsuits, filed by a continuous string of special interest groups) the cost in real dollars would be almost twenty times greater (or about $1 billion in 1915 dollars).

Elsewhere railroads expanded, new universities opened, harbors were dredged, and thousands of acres of new farmland brought into production. But, while all these developments were important, there were two mega-projects in particular that would catapult Southern California into the future and directly impact the lives of Henry and Gusty.

The first was led by Henry Huntington. Described as a visionary and philanthropist by his admirers and a scoundrel by others, Huntington was the Steve Jobs of his day—a man who could peer into the future— and for Huntington the future was electricity.[12]

In February of 1910 he began construction of the Big Creek Hydroelectric Project, which was located high in the Sierra Nevada Mountains some 250 miles north of Los Angeles. An undertaking of staggering complexity and difficulty, the first phase consisted of four dams, two power stations, and hundreds of miles of high voltage transmission lines. Seven more dams would eventually follow, but by the end of 1913 the Big Creek project was online and turning a profit.

Huntington's accomplishment quite literally brightened the prospects for Southern California (and the families of electricians

---

12 While countless "experts" claim to be able to see into the future, it's actually an extremely rare talent. As an easy example, in 2006, out of tens of thousands of bankers, economists, politicians, and investment advisors, only a handful saw the coming of the Great Recession. Or consider the sorrowful example of the McFadden brothers. In 1902, while Huntington was preparing to bet his entire fortune of the future of electricity, these guys sold Newport, Lido, and Balboa islands for $35,000.00—real estate that would soon be worth millions and a few decades after that, Billions!

like Henry Miner). However, power alone would not secure the area's future. Water—the lifeblood of cities and agriculture alike—would ultimately decide Southern California's fate.

Enter William Mulholland.

Born in Ireland in 1855, Mulholland ran away from home at age 15 and spent the next several years narrowly surviving a series of adventures and near-death experiences that read like a Hollywood movie and culminate with Mulholland as a stowaway aboard a ship in New York Harbor bound for California. Discovered a few weeks into the journey, he was abruptly put ashore in Panama, where, undeterred, he hiked across the isthmus—47 miles of yellow-fever infested jungle decades before the Panama Canal existed—made it to the Pacific Ocean, and finally arrived in Los Angeles in 1877.

He was 22 years old and, although Southern California was not his intended destination, Mulholland never left. Through a string of serendipitous encounters and opportunities he made a career out of water, or, more accurately, the distribution of water. Rising through the ranks of various water companies he became a self-taught civil engineer and, in 1902, the first superintendent of the newly formed Los Angeles Water Department.

Mullholland had long recognized that water was the key to growth, but two unsolvable problems stood in his way: first, Southern California has a simi-arid climate with unreliable rainfall, and second, the entire area is sandwiched between the Pacific Ocean on the west and, to the east (past a narrow range of coastal mountains) hundreds of miles of open desert.

If Southern California was to prosper, water would have to be found elsewhere, and Mulholland possessed both the brilliance and determination to solve the problem. Over the next decade (and with often unscrupulous tactics) he acquired the water rights to the Owens Valley and then directed the design and construction of a gravity-fed aqueduct which would carry the water 233 miles through the Sierra Nevada Mountains via 164 tunnels.

Over 30,000 people attended the opening day celebration for the Los Angeles Aqueduct on November 5, 1913.

When water from the Owens Valley reached the San Fernando Valley on November 5, 1913, Mulholland, addressing the crowd at the opening ceremony declared, "There it is. Take it."

It was an understatement nearly as epic as the achievement it represented and captures both the confidence and hubris of the day—a time when "might made right" and issues like the environment and minority interests were pushed aside.

Nevertheless, there's no denying Mulholland's accomplishments. Given an abundance of water the population of Southern California all but exploded, with the City of Los Angeles alone increasing five-fold by 1940.[13] An abundance of water also ushered in a new era in agriculture as large-scale irrigation became practical, which in turn gave rise to large farming operations that provided jobs to men like Gusty Carlson. It even helped sustain small privately held orange groves.

*   *   *   *

Other items of note during the decade of the 1910s include: the sinking of HMS Titanic, the first income tax in the U.S., and (our narrator's personal favorite) the astronomer Percival Lowell's repeated announcements that canals were being built on Mars. But, of all the tumult produced by the 1910s, World War I stands apart.

On the surface this may be surprising. The Spanish Flu, for example, killed more than twice as many people as all of World War I combined.[14] Yet, other than the immediate and obvious misery caused by those 50 million deaths, when the Spanish Flu ended in 1920 it left few consequences behind.

---

13 By 1940 the population of the City of Los Angeles stood at 1.5 million—a number slightly larger than the population of the entire state in 1900.

14 In the United States the Spanish Flu killed 6-times more Americans than World War I (675,000 vs117,000).

World War I, on the other hand, was hugely consequential. On the geopolitical stage, empires that had ruled vast portions of the globe collapsed, and across much of Eastern Europe and North Africa new nation-states rose to take their place—Finland, Poland, Hungary, Jordan, and Saudi Arabia to name a few.

World War I also significantly affected the U.S.—particularly the millions of young men in the Armed Forces. When the war broke out in 1914, the vast majority of Americans—including Congress and President Woodrow Wilson—were firmly opposed to becoming involved. In fact, Wilson won re-election in November 1916 with the slogan, "He kept us out of War."

It was a promise he would be unable to keep.

Only three months after Wilson was elected, Germany began a campaign of unrestricted submarine warfare, which quickly led to the sinking of American merchant ships. Germany well knew that these attacks would bring America into the war against them but gambled the German Army would defeat the English and French forces before American troops could arrive—a bet that nearly paid off.

At Wilson's urging Congress declared war on April 6, 1917, when the size of the entire U.S.

Iconic recruitment poster first used in World War I.

Army stood at just 127,500 vs German forces in excess of 10 million. It would take nearly a year for the U.S. to mobilize and bring sufficient men and material to Europe to help win the "War to End all Wars."

To that end, the draft was reinstated, and among the millions of young men who signed up was Oscar Carlson, Bee's oldest brother.

Likely due to mechanical skills learned on the farm, Oscar soon found himself training not with the infantry but as a mechanic with the latest weapons system of the day—the Army Air Corp's biplanes.

By the following spring, American troops were arriving in Europe at the rate of 10,000 soldiers per day, and Oscar's 1st Aero Division, was among them—reaching France in late March 1918.

Though, Oscar's assignment to the Aero Squadron would save him from the horrors of trench warfare, it hardly made him safe. From

the time his troop ship departed for France until the War ended (eight long months later) nearly an additional one-million Allied soldiers would lose their lives via submarine attacks, artillery barrages, poison gas, and disease. Moreover, American troops (and the Aero Divisions supporting them) were to find themselves in the forefront of some of the biggest battles of the War as the critical reinforcements who turned the tide in the Allie's favor.

Bee's oldest brother, Oscar Carlson, in his Army uniform, 1918.

Back home, thousands of miles away, the Carlson family could only wait and hope—their only communication with Oscar being the occasional handwritten letter, and these could take weeks or even months to arrive. Finally, on the 11th hour, of the 11th day, of the 11th month of 1918 (four years and four months after it had begun) the War ended, and shortly afterwards Oscar sent his last letter home.

It arrived in late November and told Bee and her family that Oscar had survived the War and hoped to be home soon, but since that letter there had been only silence. Was he still in France? Had his ship been lost at sea? Had he fallen ill? No one knew.

For the entire Carlson family, the weeks leading up to Christmas in 1918 began to fill with dread. With each passing day they grew ever more concerned, and by Christmas Eve everyone feared the worst. Bee's mother and father had discussed postponing the holiday altogether but decided it would be best for the rest of the family if they proceeded.

On Christmas Eve, therefore, the festivities continued as usual, but no one's heart was in it. All their thoughts and hopes and prayers were with Oscar. By early evening, with the preparations complete, they had just sat down to dinner, when there was a loud knock on the front door. Everyone ran to open it, each of them fearing it would be an Army officer with tragic news. Instead, standing in a pool of light from the open door, stood Oscar!

In a rumpled uniform and still holding onto the duffle bag he'd been carrying since leaving France, he was engulfed by the family. Smothered in hugs, kisses, and tears, Oscar eventually managed to explain that for weeks he'd been traveling by ship, by train, and by foot, always ahead of the second letter he'd sent way back in France announcing his return.

For sheer dramatic effect it's hard to improve upon Oscar's homecoming, and for Bee, who was then a freshman in high school, this would forever remain her favorite story. Interestingly, while her other childhood stories were told with some frequency, Oscar's homecoming was treated like some kind of fine china—only brought it out on special occasions. She'd carefully set the stage, fill-in all the details and always end with, "It was the best Christmas I ever had!" It surely must have been, because in each telling, when she came to the part where the family found Oscar on the front porch, Bee always burst into a smile that was so joyful it felt like the whole room was lighting up.

CHAPTER 7

Bee at a Crossroad

Bee had just turned 16 years old when the 1920s began, and the connection between those two milestones holds more irony than one might guess.

For anyone who has experienced the trails of adolescence, that transition from childhood to adulthood will likely bring back a generous helping of angst-filled memories—and so it must have been for Bee. However, for her generation there was an added twist, because throughout the 1920s

Bee's senior yearbook picture from 1922.

the entire country was having a similar angst-filled experience as it tried to navigate the cultural transition between old America and new America.

The decade opened with the 1920 census revealing for the first time in our nation's history that more Americans were living in cities than on farms, and the differences in those experiences were accelerating the divisions that plague our country to this day: traditional rural culture vs. modern urban culture (or to use more current terms: Conservatives vs. Liberals).

Incredibly, as though trying to enshrine their differences, the two camps managed to separately pass the 18th and 19th Amendments—both of which went into effect in early 1920. Prohibition, the 18th Amendment, was beloved by conservatives and the religious right, who sought to ban the sale and consumption of alcohol, while the 19th Amendment, championed by liberals, gave women the right to vote.

It's hard to overstate the differing value systems these two amendments represent, and harder still to understand how they were both able to pass. Constitutional amendments by design are supposed to reflect the values of American society—that's why they require ratification by three-quarters of the states to become law.

Imagine, then, the poor history teacher at Fullerton High School tasked with trying to explain to Bee and a classroom full of 16-year-olds what unifying theme connects them.

It doesn't work; the two amendments point the country in two different directions.

Nevertheless, Bee's teacher likely gave it his best shot. Although, as his students nodded off in confusion, one can almost hear him issuing that familiar history-teacher-warning of: "Those who cannot remember the past are condemned to repeat it."[15] However, that seems not to have worked either. Nor—and this is distressingly relevant—did

---

15 First coined by the Spanish philosopher George Santayana, versions of this quote have also been attributed to Winston Churchill, Karl Marx, and others.

it work for future generations, because a full century later America is experiencing an alarming "déjà vu all over again" of the 1920s.

Then, as now, the country was bitterly divided along several now familiar fault lines—immigration, identity politics, Prohibition (now the War on Drugs), and race—and no one better illustrates this recurring cycle than Warren Harding. The 1920 Republican Presidential Candidate, Harding won the election by encouraging a wave of isolationism with his (then original) slogan, "America First."

The 1920s also saw a sharp, and never-before-seen, rise in consumerism as improvements in manufacturing, coupled with new and easy credit, allowed the average American to purchase a myriad of products such as sewing machines, refrigerators, and most especially, automobiles.

All of this consumption, according to traditionalist, was further proof that the country was "going to Hell in a handbasket." Indeed, later historians would describe the growing conflicts between old and new America as a cultural civil war, which throughout the decade of the 1920s produced frequent and sometimes deadly battles across the country.[16]

Altogether, the 1920s would have been a challenging time for anyone to grow up, and, as we shall soon see, the Universe wasn't inclined to grant Bee any special favors.

*   *   *   *

---

16 Including the Tulsa race riots in 1921. Viewed by many historians as the single most shameful event in our nation's history, a White mob attacked and destroyed the African American neighborhood of Greenwood, leaving 300 people dead and 10,000 people homeless.

When Bee graduated from high school in June of 1922, she became the only member of her family to ever earn a diploma. Apparently, this was a particularly proud moment for her father and Bee would forever remember the smile on his face as she walked across the stage. The following September, when less than 1% of women earned a bachelor's degree, Bee entered college.

It would have been an elite group of young men and women and the excitement Bee felt for this period of her life was still evident some forty years later when she began to encourage her grandchildren's college aspirations—a cause especially dear to her heart after her own college dreams ended in tragedy.

As Gusty Carlson had sat amongst the crowd of well-wishers at Bee's high school graduation, he was seriously ill. Over the past few months he had been experiencing chronic fatigue and his symptoms were getting worse. Later that summer he was diagnosed with Pernicious Anemia—a rare disease in which the body absorbs vitamin B-12 poorly or not at all. Found almost exclusively in people of Scandinavian descent, it usually develops in late middle age, and Gusty checked both boxes. His prognosis was fatal.

He died that November and so too did Bee's dreams of college. She had just turned 18 and forever after there was a piece of Bee's soul that hurt whenever she remembered this period of her life. Obviously, the double pain of losing her father and losing her dreams of graduating from college would have been awful, but the circumstances surrounding his death soon conspired to make it even worse.

Though Gusty's death at age 57 exactly matched the average male life expectancy at the time, it was heartbreakingly unwarranted. Unbeknownst to the medical community of Southern California, the same summer Gusty received his fatal diagnosis, a doctor in San Francisco had discovered a cure for Pernicious Anemia: a diet rich in cow's liver (½ pound per day) and leafy green vegetables would return most patients to full health within weeks. A few years later vitamin B-12 was synthesized (so it could be taken as a supplement or an injectable) and the disease all but disappeared.

Looking back, one can't help but react to Gusty's death with a string of "if-only" solutions, but here's the rub: any timeline that does not see Bee enter the workforce in 1923 immediately produces an existential crisis, because most of the characters we're about to meet (including our narrator) would all disappear in a puff of logic.

Tragically, for Gusty and his immediate family, no life-saving solution presented itself. With no pension, no Social Security,[17] and (after raising six children) little savings, the family could ill afford a non-working member. At the end of her first semester Bee dropped out of college to find employment.

She was soon hired by the City of Placentia where she must have made quite an impression. Only months into her new job, at age 18, Bee became the youngest-ever acting City Clerk, when that position suddenly became available.

It was a remarkable achievement for anyone and especially for an 18-year-old single woman in the early part of the twentieth century.

---

17 Social Security didn't exist until 1935 when it was signed into law by President Franklin Roosevelt as part of the "New Deal."

Looking towards her future, Bee must have imagined a long and successful career in government ahead of her. But that's not what happened. Instead, she would soon meet a strange man who would move her future along an entirely unexpected path.

CHAPTER 8

A Strange Man

Frankly, "strange" only begins to describe my future grandfather, Abe Miner. A man of few words, much action, and a lifelong propensity to confound just about anyone who knew him, Abe could also be one of the most single-minded individuals on the planet, and in 1923, at age 21, he was on a mission to open his first business in Placentia, California.

It would be named the A.B. Miner Motor Company[18] and besides inventory, equipment, employees, and a hundred other details, Abe also needed a business license, which could only be acquired at the city clerk's office. No doubt he would have considered this bureaucratic requirement a useless and costly waste of time. He would have also been anxious to complete the process as quickly as possible and get on to other more pressing matters. He was about to change his mind.

---

18 Wanting a business name that was easy to pronounce and remember, he dropped "Alfred" and "Burrows" in favor of his initials. Soon, his employees and customers began calling him A-B which quickly morphed into Abe. The nickname stuck, and for the rest of his life he was only ever known as "Abe" (including by his children and grandchildren).

Entering City Hall and walking into the city clerk's office, Abe came face to face with Bee Carlson—the "giver of business licenses." For a bureaucrat, she was unexpectedly young and attractive, and as she helped him fill out the necessary forms, Abe quickly added "smart" and "educated" to her list of attributes. Best of all, she had an almost infectious enthusiasm for life—a quality perfectly suited to offset Abe's introverted personality and frequently gruff exterior.

Apparently, he was immediately smitten, and just as quickly his entrepreneurial side must have gone into hyperdrive. In the next few minutes, in what was perhaps the best sales pitch of his entire life, Abe not only received his new business license, but far more importantly, he had a first date.

*　*　*　*

The A.B. Miner Motor Company opened in the early years of the Roaring Twenties—a period of growth, prosperity, and more than enough unsound economic policies to ensure the Great Depression—but that financial disaster was in everyone's distant future. As a young man just starting out, all Abe could see was a "Land of Opportunity," and he was confident in his ability to succeed.

That self-assured attitude would prove to be justified. Over the course of his life, Abe would start a series of successful companies that ranged from retail to manufacturing, from service to distribution, and more than once into categories where no one had ventured before. Curiously, on the surface there doesn't seem to be any connection between Abe's various entrepreneurial adventures, and, frankly, it doesn't get any better below the surface. There were no connections except that in each case Abe was able to spot a paradigm shift before most anyone else.

By the time he liquidated his last business at age 71, Abe had started six completely different and successful companies along with a handful of "hobby businesses"—an astounding achievement when you consider that more than half of all new businesses fail within the first year.[19]

Still, Abe wasn't invincible. Twice in his career he was nearly ruined—once by the Great Depression and later by a partner. Nevertheless, he recovered both times and before reaching his 50th birthday, Abe had made enough money to comfortably retire. It didn't work. The pursuit of leisure just wasn't that interesting to him. Abe had to be doing something. More than that, he had to be accomplishing something.

Altogether, Abe wasn't just different; he was odd: an original "enigma wrapped in a paradox" kind of guy who didn't fit within any convenient labeling system. For example, driven comes easily to mind, and that would just about explain Abe's professional persona. However, that simple descriptor doesn't begin to encompass the remaining portion of his life and personality.

At work he prided himself on his appearance to the point of being vain. Pictures throughout his career consistently show him wearing a sports coat and tie, his hair combed-back and shiny with Brylcreem™

---

19 Abe's major businesses included: automobile dealership, nationwide distributor of automobile wax and polish, manganese mine, hardware store, coin and stamp shop, antique store. (Statistically, his string of successes places him in the top 1% of all would-be entrepreneurs.)

and, for at least as long as I knew him, a liberal splash of Old Spice™ after-shave. Yet, when the weekend arrived, he escaped into an old pair of canvas pants, a flannel shirt, and the great outdoors. He was an uncommonly talented salesman who could engage anyone in conversation but remained terrified of public speaking his entire life. Most perplexing of all, however—in a life already filled with incongruities—was his relationship with addiction. For most of his adult life Abe was a severe alcoholic. Then, one afternoon in his late 50s, he decided to quit drinking. He didn't announce it. He didn't talk about it afterwards. He just quit.

In short, he was a man with enormous talents and abundant flaws, and the resulting internal conflicts caused by those forces never seemed to allow him much in the way of inner peace. But then, Abe never appeared to be much interested in inner peace. He was always too busy making his latest project successful. Seriously, if it had ever occurred to Abe to stop and smell the roses (which is unlikely), he would have immediately wanted to know how many roses the other guy had smelled and who was ahead.

Any way you looked at it, Abe was a force unto himself, and his unusual blend of personality and talents produced a series of professional accomplishments that were downright astonishing. His personal life, I'm afraid, was more of a mixed bag; yet, even in this he would eventually enjoy a good measure of success.

Of course, no one succeeds in a vacuum. Certainly, talent and determination play leading roles, but behind every successful person lies a measure of luck and a measure of help from others. Abe was no exception, and what had to be the luckiest day in his life began to unfold when he walked into City Hall on that fateful day in 1923. He couldn't have known how vital Bee Carlson would be to his life's successes, but, to his credit, Abe always had the sense to recognize a good deal when he saw it. On that morning it took him only a few minutes to decide that Bee was the "best deal" he'd ever seen.

CHAPTER 9

Abe and Bee

Their first date must have gone well, because after a short courtship, Abe and Bee were married on October 23, 1923 (the day after Bee's 19th birthday). Three years later she was pregnant with their first child, Lee (my father). Tragically, a second son died in childbirth and a third from whooping cough just before his first birthday. Finally, in 1932, a fourth son, Glenn, survived.

On the domestic side Abe and Bee's marriage was fairly traditional, meaning Bee did almost all of the cooking, cleaning, and childcare—all typical responsibilities of wives in early twentieth century America. In nearly everything else, however, she would prove to be almost as odd as her new husband.

As a young bride and mother in her twenties, for example, Bee wore pants almost every day, decades before they were fashionable. In her free time, while other women might be socializing at tea parties, Bee was more likely to be found far offshore on a fishing boat when the albacore were running or crouched in a hunting blind waiting for the sun to rise and the geese to fly overhead.

In countless other examples Bee's behavior was often at odds with the norm, but (and this is the clever bit) often not for the reasons everyone assumed. She wore pants, for instance, not as a fashion or political statement, but simply because they were practical and comfortable. She never cared what anyone thought about them.

Fishing was straightforward: she loved every part of the sport and old pictures show her, with rod and reel in hand, fishing in freshwater, saltwater, on boats, in the surf, and alongside rivers. Hunting, however, was an altogether different situation and one that offers a delightful insight into how Bee's mind worked.

Abe and the boys were passionate about bird hunting and Bee regularly accompanied them. For thirty-plus years she tromped through fields under a blazing sun and 100-degree temperatures looking for pheasants; she endured days of icy winds and frozen ground waiting for a flock of Canadian honkers to fly overhead, and she hiked untold miles over hills and through brush-covered ravines looking for quail.

But, in all that time Bee rarely hit anything. Time after time Abe and the boys would limit out, while Bee came up emptyhanded, and everyone assumed she was just an unusually poor marksman.

Everyone was wrong.

Years after Abe died, when Bee was well into her seventies, she quietly admitted that in all her hunting adventures she had deliberately aimed her 4-10 shotgun *behind* the birds.

"I just didn't want to kill anything," she explained simply. For Bee hunting was never about birds, or shotguns, or limits. Hunting was a cover story, an excuse to be with her family.

But as odd as her private life might have been, it was her professional life that most clearly broke the molds society had prepared for her. At a time when few women (especially married women) worked outside the home, Bee traded her career in government for a career in business, where her skills soon proved indispensable to the A.B. Miner Motor Company.

Certainly, Abe remained the leader and visionary in all their business ventures, but without Bee, Abe's string of successes would have been unlikely. Within their partnership Bee filled two vital roles. First, she was the "numbers" person. To her fell the often dull but crucial details of bookkeeping, payroll, inventory, and the like. Second, though at least as important, Bee was extraordinarily good with people. Whether it was employees, customers, or suppliers, everyone loved her.

As individuals Abe and Bee were uncommonly different, but perhaps the oddest thing about them was that they managed to survive as a couple. Abe was the archetypal introverted thinker, while Bee landed on the opposite side of that spectrum as an extroverted feeler. Any student of Organizational Theory would have pronounced a pairing of those conflicting personality types as being fatal. Extroverts and introverts will usually drive one another crazy, while thinkers and feelers typically have such difficulty communicating with one another they soon quit trying.

Yet despite those formidable differences, at the core of their being Abe and Bee shared a handful of crucial values: family was important, hard work was honorable, and financial success was a personal responsibility. Perhaps more importantly, they seemed early on to have appreciated each other's strengths, and their life-long partnership worked remarkably well. For forty-seven years, until Abe's death in 1974, and through a multitude of different businesses and adventures, the two of them were seldom apart.

CHAPTER 10

The Roaring '20s

Sadly, few family stories survive from this period and none at all that relate to (my great-grandparents) Henry and Bessie[20]—their hopes and dreams, their interests and talents, have all been lost. Nevertheless, sleuthing through the available public records does provide at least a sketch of my great-grandfather.

Like his father before him Henry seemed intent on avoiding routine. After moving his family to Brea in 1910, he changed professions on at least three occasions, including becoming a general contractor before eventually returning to what was apparently his first love, farming. He also appears to have speculated in real estate—owning several different homes spread across Southern California. Most heartening of all, though, is that Abe and Bee chose "Henry" as

---

20 Save the single memory I have of once meeting Bessie in the early 1960s when I was about nine years old. She was introduced as "Ganny"—a name affectionately given to her by her grandchildren. Already in her late 80s, she was the oldest, tiniest, and frailest looking human being I'd ever encountered. When it was suggested that I give my great-grandmother a hug, I carefully bent over (she was that short) and put one arm gently around her shoulder—afraid that if I squeezed too hard she'd break in two.

the middle name of their first-born child, and there's simply no way they would have made that choice unless the original Henry was a decent human being.

But all that aside, the supposition that most affects our story is that Henry and Bessie must have enjoyed enough financial success to lend Abe the money necessary to open his first business, because no bank—then or now—would ever provide a large unsecured loan to an inexperienced 21-year-old.

When Abe opened for business in 1923, automobiles had been around for 20 years and Ford Motor Company, with its Model T, dominated the industry. Introduced in 1909 at a sales price of $825, the Model T was an immediate success. And then it got better. Much better. By 1924, owing to vast improvements in productivity, the price reached a low of just $265.00 (about $4,000 in 2020 dollars), and Ford was selling 2,000,000 vehicles per year—more than double all other automobile manufacturers combined.

The A.B. Miner Motor Company, circa 1925.
Abe and Bee are standing far right.

**The
Ten-Millionth**

Ford

The 10,000,000th Ford car left
the Highland Park factories
of the Ford Motor Company
June 4. This is a production
achievement unapproached in
automotive history. Tremen-
dous volume has been the out-
growth of dependable, convenient, economical service.

Ford Motor Company

The Touring Car
$295

Newspaper ad from 1924.

For Abe this would have been a perfectly delightful situation—selling cars almost as fast as you could get them—but he wasn't that lucky. Ford wasn't looking for young inexperienced dealers, which meant that Abe had to align with one of the second-tier manufacturers like Studebaker, Hudson, DeSoto, and dozens more. By accident or design he chose wisely with Chevrolet.

That said, the wisdom of Abe's decision would not have been apparent in 1923, and it would have looked worse still in 1924, when Ford outsold Chevrolet by a factor of 10 to 1. However, as the decade advanced Chevrolet's sales increased dramatically while Ford—blinded by its own success—began to stumble.

Competing on price had always been Ford's winning strategy, but early in its history General Motors made the successful (and therefore brilliant) decision not to play that game. Instead, they stressed *features and benefits*. So, where Ford offered the Model T in "any color you wanted as long as it was black" Chevrolet offered consumers a choice of multiple colors. They were also the first to offer an electric ignition (instead of a hand-crank) and began early on to experiment with style.

It proved a winning strategy and by the end of 1928 General Motors had surpassed Ford in sales.

Today Ford's blunder is required reading for any student of marketing, and forever after advertising campaigns have rarely ventured far from GM's time-honored script of selling features and benefits rather than price. But, for all the kudos GM's Marketing Department earned, it was another department altogether that would prove to be the most impactful: Finance.

Although the price of a new automobile was becoming ever more affordable, few would-be buyers had that much cash on hand. So, in 1919 (a decade before Ford figured it out) GM began financing new purchases through an installment sale (i.e. monthly payments).

Interestingly, this was hardly a new idea—Singer Sewing Machines, for example, had been offering monthly payments to their customers since before the Civil War—but it wasn't until the 1920's that the idea really took off, when industry began offering washing machines, refrigerators, automobiles and more for a "low monthly payment."

Even more impactful (for the overall economy) was a new form of financing developed for the stock market, where buying "on margin" allowed investors to purchase stock in a company for 10%–20% down and the balance paid back with future profits.

All together installment sales and buying stocks on margin proved to be self-fulfilling marvels: as consumer spending increased, factories hired more workers, which increased payrolls, which led to more purchasing of goods and stocks, which sent the Stock Market soaring to new highs. For almost the entirety of the 1920s most Americans felt like they were riding some kind of economic magic carpet toward ever increasing prosperity.

But there was a problem. Lulled by nearly a decade of rising sales, profits, and stock prices, nearly everyone forgot two fundamental truths: a) 20% annual growth is unsustainable; and, b) if something can't go on forever, it won't. Near the end of 1929 the economic boom of the 1920s ended in a cataclysmic bust.

CHAPTER 11

The Great Depression

Even today, despite all our hard-won knowledge and impressive technology, no society, government, or economic system has ever figured out how to avoid boom and bust cycles—the Great Recession of 2007-2009 being the most recent proof. In fact, throughout the 20th century the U.S. stock market averaged a major downturn about every five years. However, nothing before or since has ever rivaled the crash of 1929.

By mid-November of that year, when the stock market had lost almost half its value, President Hoover's administration decided to intervene. Against the advice of most economists the Treasury Department implemented a stanchly conservative agenda of dramatically increased tariffs, higher interest rates, and reduced lending—exactly the opposite of what was needed—and made everything worse. Much worse.

The slide continued through the summer of 1932, when the Stock Market closed at its lowest value of the twentieth century (89% below its peak in 1929) a point so low that it would take decades to climb back to its pre-crash numbers—finally equaling its 1929 peak in 1954.

Today, it's hard to appreciate how frighteningly bad the Great Depression really was. Businesses by the tens of thousands went bankrupt (along with more than 5,000 banks). Unemployment exceeded 25%. Even more haunting was the toll it took on families. Facing homelessness and starvation, parents abandoned 150,000 children to orphanages and twice that many to foster care.

DIMES

For those who lived through it, The Great Depression left a mark: an indelible first-person experience that one's financial security could be taken away by uncontrollable forces.

Even decades later and despite constant reassurances by learned economists and confident government officials that the Great Depression could never happen again, those who lived through it *knew* differently.

Still, that didn't stop me trying to explain it all to my father shortly after I'd finished my first economics class in college.

He listened politely and responded that, while all the economic theory I'd learned was interesting, it didn't account for the fact that, as a little boy growing up in the 1930s, he'd watched factory workers (the lucky few who still had a job) line up on Fridays to be paid for a week's worth of work *with a stack of dimes*.

For the automobile industry the Great Depression was catastrophic. Sales of new Chevrolet automobiles fell by more than half in 1931 and then by half again in 1932 (a total decline of 75% below their peak in 1929). For most dealerships it was a fatal two years and so it proved for the A.B. Miner Motor Company.

This period would mark the low point of Abe's life—a time he and Bee rarely talked about and then only in broad brushstrokes. With his first business ending in failure, little to no prospect of finding a job, and the added responsibility of a brand-new baby (Glenn, born 1932), the future could hardly have looked bleaker.

There's no record of how many plans Abe hatched or dead-end leads he followed, but by 1933, in the midst of all the ruin around him, he somehow discovered Kolor-Kote.

In those days. automobile paint didn't last nearly as long as the automobile itself. The paint faded quickly and had to be constantly waxed to protect it from the elements. To solve that deficiency, a chemist in Culver City, California, had developed a two-step process that first applied pigment to the oxidized paint surface and then sealed it with a new and long-lasting wax. The results were all but magical—an old automobile treated with Kolor-Kote really did look brand new.

However, despite Kolor-Kote's effectiveness as a product, it was failing in the marketplace: slowly being killed by the inventor's lack of business skills.

It's not clear how the two men connected or what persuasive argument Abe employed, but they ended up forming a partnership: the inventor would manage production, while Abe assumed responsibility for sales and distribution.

It was slow going at first, with Abe and Bee both selling and applying the product. However, by the mid 1930s, Kolor-Kote's sales were growing so rapidly that Abe was able to catch the attention of Chevrolet.

Invited to make a presentation, Abe must have given the performance of a lifetime, because Chevrolet decided to test Kolor-Kote at dealerships across Southern California. The product sold well and within a few months Chevrolet wanted Kolor-Kote distributed nationwide.

For Abe and Bee, it was the chance of a lifetime. Sales were growing exponentially, and they soon decided to move their operation (and family) to Atlanta, Georgia—a more central location from which they could better oversee their growing sales and distribution network. Remember, this was before most people had a (landline) telephone. Nor did commercial air travel or overnight shipping yet exist. Only trains could move passengers and freight over long distance, and the only alternative to face-to-face communication was the U.S. Mail or, if it was really urgent, a telegram.

Atlanta was everything they could have hoped for. Kolor-Kote was flourishing, and their new home bordered on glorious—a mini-mansion from the antebellum period, complete with magnificent oak trees, a shaded front porch, and broad green lawns in every direction. Inside, the house boasted large rooms, fine furniture, wood floors, and, best of all for Bee, a live-in maid and nanny.

Bee would later describe those years in Atlanta as something right out of *Gone with the Wind*. Sadly, it turned out, she was referring to the *entire* book, because after those bucolic opening chapters—full of loveliness and promise—their time in Atlanta would give way to conflict and destruction.

Abe and Bee, circa 1935.

Back in California, their inventor/partner was becoming increasingly militant in his efforts to renegotiate their agreement and gain a greater share of Kolor-Kote's profits. Disinclined to give away what they had worked so hard to create, Abe and Bee resisted, and the partnership erupted into full-scale conflict. With Abe and Bee controlling sales and distribution, the inventor fought back through his control of production—first by shipping incomplete orders and later by shipping defective product.

It was a doomsday strategy only the deranged would follow, which, tragically, soon proved to be the salient point. The inventor, whose irrational behavior was already causing near fatal injury to Kolor-Kote, finished the job by committing suicide and taking the secret formula with him.

The business collapsed almost overnight.

It was a devastating loss, especially for Abe. Indeed, one can only begin to appreciate the ruin of Kolor-Kote when juxtaposed against the accomplishment it represented—i.e., that in any given generation only a handful of entrepreneurs are ever able to create a nation-wide business from scratch.

Surely, a long period of mourning was in order, but this was late 1939 and the U.S. economy, which had finally begun a modest recovery in 1933, had once again fallen back into recession. Self-pity wasn't going to pay the bills. Instead, Abe cast about looking for a new opportunity and came up with something no one (and I really mean no one) could have guessed.

CHAPTER 12

Miners in the Mojave

Throughout the 1930s, while most Americas clung to a policy of isolationism, the stage was being set for World War II. Fascist dictators rose to power in Spain, Italy, and Germany, while in the Far East, Japan seized Manchuria, Korea, and much of China.

Yet, despite all the warning signs Congress remained unmoved. Even after the Nazi invasion of Poland and the low countries, the fall of France, and the threatened invasion of Great Britain, Congress persisted in its naïve belief that American Neutrality would somehow protect the Country.

Fortunately, President Franklin Delano Roosevelt (FDR) faced the facts head-on, recognized the danger, and acted on multiple fronts to prepare the Nation for war.

Specifically, he helped negotiate the sales of aircraft to Great Britain (which helped kick-start American companies like Boeing and Lockheed into production before Pearl Harbor) and began supplying ships through the Lend-Lease Program—both were famously effective. But, as headline-grabbing as events in Europe were at this time—Mussolini, Hitler, the Battle of Britain, and so-on—the War Department was becoming increasingly worried about Japan.

Tragically, they failed to anticipate Japan's attack on Pearl Harbor; however, by the late 1930s the War Department couldn't help but recognize that Japanese conquests in the Far East were cutting off America's access to strategic materials. Chief among these was rubber,[21] but the list also included metals like tin, chromite, and manganese.

Improbably, it is to this last item, manganese, that our story turns to next.

Though making up only 1% of steel (98%+ is iron), manganese is the critical alloy that makes steel "hard" and, from the ruins of his Kolor-Kote operation in Atlanta, Abe learned of the War Department's new-found demand for this strategic metal. Connecting the dots, he found an abandoned manganese mine in the Mojave Desert, where, in his third career move and a remarkable pun on the family name, Abe became an actual miner.

He didn't know the first thing about mining and, according to Bee's later account, he rather underestimated the hardships of living in the deep desert. But what Abe did know was critical: one doesn't make money *extracting* manganese ore; one makes money *selling* manganese ore. Abe knew how to sell, and by 1940 he had leveraged that talent into a contract with the U.S. government to supply all the high-grade manganese ore he could find.

*   *   *   *

---

21 No military vehicle could operate without rubber parts. A medium-sized tank, for example, used 1,500 pounds of the stuff, and a battleship more than 68 tons!

Perhaps if you were like Abe and had grown up near Miner County, South Dakota, the Mojave Desert wouldn't look all that inhospitable. At least you weren't likely to die in a snowstorm there. But for anyone else—let's say his wife and two sons, for example—it must have looked and felt like something out of Dante's *Inferno*.

With apologies for now having twice insulted the good people of Miner County, our narrator is reluctant to add injury to the stalwart residents of Blythe, California. However, having visited both locations, he can tell you (with feeling) that Miner County—with its featureless landscape, winter blizzards, and scorching summers—is, in fact, a paradise on Earth compared to Blythe.

Blythe is in the middle of the Mojave Desert, where winter temperatures can be 100 degrees at noon before plunging to below freezing at night, and summer temperatures can reach 130 degrees in the shade (assuming, of course, one can find shade).

So, basically, it's hot and unpleasant in the winter (except when it's freezing) and miserably hot and unpleasant all the rest of the year—which is pretty much all there is to know about the place. Nevertheless—in a nod to journalistic balance—a few details of marginal historical interest are included below.

Much like the town of Huron, Blythe is an unintended consequence of railroads and geography. In the early 1900s, and for reasons that must have made sense at the time, the Atchison, Topeka and Santa Fe Railway decided it would be easier to go *through* the Mojave Desert rather than around it. This required crossing the Colorado River at some point, and that intersection—first inhabited by a small handful of long-suffering cattle ranchers—eventually became the town of Blythe.

Slowly the town grew and by 1940, when the Miner Family arrived, the population had swelled to some 2,000 hapless souls who had (one can only presume) arrived trailing a string of bad decisions behind them.

Now, imagine yourself having just left a beautiful home and urban lifestyle in green, tree-covered Atlanta, Georgia. Stepping off the train at Blythe Junction into the heat and the dust, a quick reconnoiter confirms that you've arrived in the middle of godforsaken nowhere. But it's much worse than that. Your new home isn't what might pass for a cute little bungalow in downtown Blythe; it's a mining shack located at the end of a dirt road that departs from the town of godforsaken nowhere before wandering some 30 miles into the open desert.

Personally, I'm not sure despair would quite cover my feelings at that point, but the A.B. Miner Family seems to have taken the whole thing in stride. Abe was more determined than ever to succeed, and Bee (who could have given lessons to the Stoics) remained her unflappable self, while the boys—Lee (my future father) and Glenn (my future uncle)—thought the whole thing looked like an adventure.

For the boys, life in the desert often was an adventure, but, before we get to some of their escapades, we should first turn our attention toward a most unexpected event—one that would see the Miner Family's life in the desert suddenly intersect with forces that would change the course of World War II.

*   *   *   *

On December 7, 1941, the Japanese attacked Pearl Harbor and America was forced into World War II. Woefully unprepared the United States (along with its major ally Great Britain) would suffer grievously for most of 1942: in the Far East, the entire U.S. Army force protecting the Philippines—23,000 American soldiers—were either killed or captured; in the Battle of the Atlantic, German U-boats were sinking British and American supply ships faster than they could be replaced; and, in North Africa, Rommel's string of victories against the British seemed unstoppable.

Yet, even as the Allies were enduring a string of defeats, the American public responded with a shared determination to fight back. From across the country, men and women volunteered for service faster than the Armed Forces could accept them, while industry rapidly switched to producing war material—less than three months after Pearl Harbor, for example, both Ford and GM had switched their entire production to jeeps, tanks, trucks, planes and more.

B-24 Bombers on Assembly Line at Ford Motor Company Willow Run Bomber Plant in Michigan, January 1943. Massively more complicated than an automobile (1,550,000 parts vs. 15,000 parts) Ford nevertheless managed to produce a B-24 bomber every 63 minutes before the war's end. (From the Collections of The Henry Ford. Gift of Ford Motor Company.)

Back in Pearl Harbor the U.S. Navy's recovery bordered on the miraculous. Certainly, the Japanese attack had been devastating—21 ships damaged or destroyed (including eight battleships). However, in less than three months, 10 of the stricken vessels had been refloated. More critically, the Navy's three aircraft carriers—having been at sea during the Japanese attack—remained undamaged and ready to fight.

For the U.S. Army, the task at hand was monumental. By the war's end more than 8 million men and women would be serving in the Army, but in the year before Pearl Harbor that number stood at just 269,093. Moreover, the U.S. was now in a two-front war—one across the Atlantic, the other on the far side of the Pacific—and at the beginning of World War II the Army completely lacked the shipping necessary to transport large numbers of troops across either ocean.

Undeterred, within weeks of entering the war, the U.S. Army began preparations for its first battle against the Germans.

Code named *Operation Torch*, General George Patton was to land in North Africa with 35,000 American Troops and capture Casablanca—the largest city and best seaport in Morocco. It was a bold plan that would require transporting an entire army—along with all their equipment and supplies—across the Atlantic Ocean and landing them on multiple beachheads.

In terms of risk and complexity, it was beyond anything the U.S. Army had ever attempted, but of all the moving parts necessary for success, Patton understood that training his unseasoned troops to fight in the harsh and unforgiving deserts of North Africa would be the most critical. For that purpose, he needed the meanest, nastiest, and most remote real estate the U.S. had to offer.

Not surprisingly, he chose the Mojave Desert.

Early 1942, therefore, came as something of a shock to the Miner Family when Patton's army began arriving only a few miles from their mining camp. Having lived for more than a year in the isolation only hundreds of miles of open desert can provide, the boys (then ages 10 and 15) were awestruck as multiple tent cities sprang up almost overnight. Across the desert a steady stream of trucks, jeeps, and tanks sped in every direction, while in the distance the sound of machine gun fire, artillery explosions, and the howling of fighter planes overhead could be heard almost daily.

For Abe and Bee, it must have been a powerful reminder of just how *real* this war had become and how close in age their oldest son was to the army of young soldiers that surrounded them. Across the globe American servicemen and women were already dying by the thousands, and no one knew what the future would bring or how the war would end.

For Lee and Glenn, though, Patton's army and all the activity it produced was seen simply as an exciting diversion from the unchanging drudgery of digging up manganese ore and loading it into boxcars … day, after day, after day.

Unhappily, for the boys it was a short-lived interruption, and by the fall of 1942—four months after they'd arrived—Patton's army and all their equipment were gone. Life at the mining camp returned to normal.

Of course, we're once again taking liberties with "normal"—a word rarely associated with living in the deep desert. However, for Lee and Glenn the mining camp was *home,* making it the only normal they knew, and between there and the 30-mile road to godforsaken nowhere, they experienced all the passages of adolescence—their first job, their first date, and, in what best captures this entire period: their first car.

With no school bus serving the deep desert, Abe and Bee were left to provide transportation to and from school for the boys. However, the hour-plus long drive to town presented something of a problem. Chauffeuring them was impractical, so, when school started in the fall of 1940, Abe purchased an old Ford coupe and taught Lee (who had just turned 14) how to drive. A year later, at age 10, Glenn became the second driver.

For the next few years the boys commuted to and from school in a car with no radio, heater, or air conditioner. The roof was black fabric that baked in the summer and did little to keep out the wind and cold of winter. Naturally, there were no seatbelts.

On winter mornings, which hovered in the low 30 degrees, they bundled up with extra clothes, blankets, and scarves. Summer afternoons were unbearably hot and always there was dust. For a few days each spring and autumn it must have been pleasant, but typically the conditions varied between freezing and baking—often in the same day. Nevertheless, and in the true spirit of what boyhood is all about, they found ways to entertain themselves.

As the 30-mile dirt road from the mine finally approached Blythe, it wandered through some actual farmland next to the Colorado River. Here the crops received water from a network of canals, which the road crossed at several points. This meant that on a typical 100+ degree afternoon one could leap into the canal fully clothed from atop Bridge "A," float a few hundred yards downstream to emerge at Bridge "B" –

where one's brother and the car would be waiting—and be completely dry in minutes.

For refreshing summertime entertainment nothing beat canal jumping, but the boys' favorite activity happened deeper into the desert. At that time jackrabbits were considered vermin. They ate crops, carried disease, procreated like, well, rabbits, and generally made a nuisance of themselves. Dispatching them was therefore considered a public service. At least that's the way the Miner Boys understood the ecosystem of their day.

It was this spirit of community service (through vermin elimination) that led Lee and Glenn to frequently go hunting on the way home from school. Once safely off the paved road and into the desert, they'd take turns behind the wheel or riding shotgun—except that in their version the passenger riding shotgun was actually armed with a lever action 22-gauge rifle. Bouncing along the desert road in the late afternoon, the boys would watch an almost endless supply of jack rabbits dart between boulders, bushes, and rabbit holes. It was like a live action shooting gallery except the shooter, who leaned far out the passenger side window and blasted away, was moving almost as much as the targets.

Today, of course, shooting jackrabbits under any conditions will get one shunned by most every portion of society (not to mention probable incarceration by the U.S Fish and Wildlife Service); but, I must confess there's still a piece of my little-boy-brain, probably dating from the Neanderthal Period, that thinks shooting real bullets at real moving targets from the window of a real moving car would be just about the most fun anyone could have. (The rest of me claims to be completely appalled by the idea.)

A MINER SIDE NOTE

LEE'S MARKSMANSHIP

The desert shooting gallery would hone Dad's marksmanship to Olympic potential. Honestly, to this day I've never met anyone who could outshoot him.

In one instance, when Dad was in his late 30s and I was about 11, we, along with another father-son team, were on a dove hunt. As the other father drove us down a bumpy tree-lined dirt road in a Jeep with no roof, Dad was riding shotgun both literally and figuratively, which meant he was sitting on the passenger side holding his shotgun with the butt resting on his right leg and the barrel pointed safely skyward.

Suddenly, Dad looked up, chambered a round, drew a short arc through the air with his barrel and fired. In a panic, the other father slammed on the brakes just as a dove (which nobody else had seen) fell to the ground. With as much nonchalance as he could manage, Dad turned to me in the back seat and said, "Hey, Mike, can you get that for me?"

It was awesome!

*   *   *   *

I first heard my father's tales of canal jumping and rabbit shooting during my own childhood, and they remained wonderful fodder for a host of my boyhood fantasies. However, along with those marvelous tales of derring-do, I also remember feeling rather uneasy when the stories ventured to encounters with wandering coyotes, scorpions that hid in your shoes at night, and rattlesnakes that lurked anyplace they could find shade. The bit about summer temperatures so hot that a piece of metal left in the sun would instantly burn your hand if you touched it without wearing gloves seemed pretty gruesome as well.

Nevertheless, there was one near-death story, frequently told by my uncle, Glenn, that I particularly enjoyed.

It was a typical summer day at the mine, which meant it was sunny, dry, and hot. It also meant that Lee and Glenn were working along with everybody else at the mining camp. Their jobs varied with the seasons and with their age. They might help fill one of the trucks with manganese ore, or (as they got older) drive the loaded truck to the railroad spur where it was dumped into railroad cars waiting to be shipped. More often they moved tools and equipment, including dynamite and blasting caps, to wherever they were needed.

Whatever the task, when the noon whistle blew, everyone headed to the cook shack, where lunch was served on wooden tables under a covered porch that allowed a short respite from the blazing sun. It also afforded a view of the entire camp, which included the nearby communal outhouse, and it was this particular structure that Lee, who was about 15 at the time, had just entered.

Unbeknownst to all, however, the outhouse was already occupied by a large rattlesnake, which had only recently arrived to enjoy the shade. According to Glenn, Lee had just sat down when he heard the unmistakable sound of the rattler behind him. Terrified, he jumped up and ran out the door, forgetting that his pants were around his ankles. He took one step, fell out of the outhouse, and landed in a heap half-naked in full view of all the workers. He had managed to escape the rattlesnake, but the poor guy's mortification was nearly fatal.

*　*　*　*

To be fair, there were aspects of the desert that could be lovely—Joshua trees silhouetted in the moonlight, a brief display of wildflowers after a rare rainstorm, or (Bee's favorite) a night sky so clear you could easily see your way by starlight. But the inescapable fact remained that everyday life in the desert was difficult, dangerous, and habitually unpleasant. Nevertheless, for most of four long years, that's where the Miner Family lived.

Every night they came home to a mining shack—a simple wood-frame building that lacked virtually every amenity one normally associates with a house. Naturally, there was no telephone or TV, but that hardly mattered, because electricity was only available for a few hours each day when the generator was running. The toilet was an outhouse and the kitchen lived next door in the shared cook shack. Every drop of water had to be trucked in.

In many ways the mining camp resembled life in a Third World country—little infrastructure, few conveniences, and an ongoing struggle for survival. However, in terms of location, it achieved what might best be described as otherworldliness—as if the 30-mile dirt road served as a gateway to a secret and solitary outpost on Mars. In every direction all one could see was dirt, tumbleweeds, cactus, and a piece of the road that led to the town of godforsaken nowhere.

There were no children living next door. There were no adult couples down the street. Month after month, season after season, the only neighbors the Miner Family ever encountered were the small group of men working the mine—a motley crew of drifters, loaners, and misfits, who worked hard, drank often, and left frequently to seek employment elsewhere.

But the most inexplicable part of the Miner Family's years in the Mojave Desert was how nonchalant they all were about it. There was a shared calmness to their storytelling, an understated matter-of-factness that was impossible to square with the sum of their experience.

As a case in point: my brother (who was never able to wrap his head around life in the desert either) once asked Bee about the many hardships she faced during those years. She seemed almost confused by the question but after some reflection finally offered, "Well, I didn't particularly like driving the dynamite truck."

Really?

Part of the mining crew, circa 1942. (Abe, center, sitting inside vehicle.)

I mean seriously, assuming one possess at least an average appreciation for personal safety (and I'm thinking here of our narrator), the idea of driving an old 1930s truck—a vehicle with primitive suspension, no shock absorbers, and loaded with thousands of pounds of dynamite—isn't just unnerving: it's unfathomable.

Honestly, the years spent by the Miner Family in the Mojave Desert always reminded me of something right out of the Old Testament. Eventually, I was sure, one of my grandparents would let slip the time Moses wandered into camp asking for directions, or mention something about a burning bush, or maybe a plague of locusts. (Although now that I think about it, it's doubtful any of those biblical events would have been noteworthy enough to be mentioned.) Regardless, I can tell you that each time I heard one of their stories about the mind-numbing, spirit-draining, death-defying years at the manganese mine, I'd scratch my head and wonder quietly to myself if maybe I'd been adopted.

CHAPTER 13

Casablanca

In the last days of 1942, the future of the world quite literally hung in the balance. Japan, having routed the Americans in the Philippines and the British at Singapore, was now threatening Australia. In Europe the German occupation was entering its third year, while Hitler's armies controlled North Africa and were mercilessly advancing into Russia.

Yet, amidst the defeats and uncertainty, by the end of 1942, the tide of war was slowly turning in the Allies favor. In the Pacific, in what would prove to be one of the most decisive battles of World War II, the U.S. Navy had defeated a much larger Japanese force at Midway Island. In the Atlantic, new weapons and new tactics were proving effective against the U-Boat menace, while, from air bases across Great Britain, American Air Crews and bombers had joined the war over occupied Europe.

Best of all, for the moral of the American people, all those troops who had trained in the Mojave Desert with General Patton had successfully landed in North Africa and by mid-November were advancing against Germany's Afrika Korps.

It was with renewed hope and optimism, therefore, that President Roosevelt gathered with his trusted inner circle at the White House to celebrate New Year's Eve. As part of the festivities an advanced copy of the new movie *Casablanca* (due to be released the following month, in late January 1943) was shown after dinner, and Roosevelt eagerly joined his guests for the evening's entertainment—believing that he alone understood the dramatic irony it represented.

He was only half right.

Two weeks later, at a Top-Secret conference, Roosevelt would meet with British Prime Minister Winston Churchill in the very same city of Casablanca. However, what neither Roosevelt nor anyone else guessed was how dangerously close life was about to imitate art.

As depicted in the movie, Casablanca was rife with intrigue. American troops had only held the city for two months, and General Patton was nearly apoplectic upon learning that he would be responsible for the safety of the two most important men on the planet. Knowing that Casablanca still held a plentiful assortment of Nazi spies and sympathizers, along with an equally plentiful assortment of thugs and criminals, Patton urged Roosevelt and Churchill to depart immediately, explaining "…the Germans are only 200 miles away and they damn sure know how to hit this place with their bombers."

Just as Patton had feared, Nazi spies almost immediately discovered Roosevelt and Churchill's presence in Casablanca and sent the information by secret cable to Berlin. Incredibly, when the message was decoded, "Casablanca" was transcribed literally as "White House" leading the German high command to believe the Allied leaders were in Washington DC.

It was a close call and a telling example of how precarious the U.S. position was throughout those first years of the war. Nevertheless, the Allies would eventually prevail. Supplied by the might of American industry, the influx of American troops, and helped by more blunders on the enemies' side than our own, the war turned increasingly in the Allies' favor. By 1944 both the German and Japanese forces had been driven into an endgame of defense and retreat.

Tragically, the slaughter and destruction would continue for another year and a half, but the end of the war was in sight, and back home—after four long years in the Mojave Desert—Abe recognized the era of the manganese mine was coming to a close.

From a strictly financial perspective, the family's years at the mining camp had been entirely successful. It hadn't made them rich, but it was enough to allow Abe and Bee considerable latitude as they pondered their next career move—unaware that their oldest son, Lee, was about to begin forging his own future.

CHAPTER 14

Lee

The months surrounding Lee's 17th birthday (June 1944) were to become more consequential than anyone, least of all Lee himself, could have foreseen, when a string of mostly poor choices (on his part) steered his life directly into the conflagration of World War II.

It began with a high school fight towards the end of his junior year. Typically, this sort of unruly behavior would have resulted in detention or perhaps a short suspension. However, rather than a fellow student, Lee's opponent had been the vice principal, and, to make it all much worse, Lee had landed at least one good punch.

Not surprisingly, the Blythe School Administration took this incident rather seriously and quickly resolved the "problem of Lee" by immediately and permanently expelling him.

From Lee's viewpoint this solution was entirely satisfactory—he had never been much of a student—but it proved surprisingly unacceptable to his parents, who, with some considerable effort, managed to implement a plan for his continuing education.

Only months before, Abe and Bee had purchased a retail building in the downtown area of Culver City, which included an upstairs apartment. This new address was now pressed into service as their primary residence, allowing Lee and Glenn to attend the local Culver City Schools.

Summer and school vacations were still spent back at the mine, but by the fall of 1944, the boys were returned to civilization. It must have been a welcome change, and Lee began to excel athletically at Hamilton High, where he took first place at the inter-city track meet by jumping 6 feet, 2 inches—a new school record that stood for many years.

Unfortunately, his performance in track and field wasn't exactly mirrored in his academic experience, where a lack of interest and effort combined to produce enough failing grades that he dropped

Lee Miner in his Navy uniform, 1945.

out of high school halfway through his senior year. With no diploma and no job, Lee decided to join the Army.

Following in the footsteps of his Uncle Oscar (Bee's brother, who had returned home so dramatically on Christmas Eve back in 1919), he opted for the Air Corps, except that Lee wanted to *fly* airplanes rather than repair them.

He was too late. The war in Europe was winding down and the demand for new pilots had ended. So, in April of 1945 (still age 17), Lee enlisted in the Navy, where, immediately after finishing boot camp, he joined hundreds of thousands of new recruits training for the invasion and occupation of the Japanese home islands.

This was infinitely more terrifying than it probably sounds. The war in the Pacific had by this time achieved a ferociousness in which no quarter was asked or given, and Lee was only weeks away from boarding a troop ship bound for the front lines.

Casualty estimates ran into the millions.

Instead, on August 6 and 9, 1945, separate atomic bombs were dropped over Hiroshima and Nagasaki. Japan surrendered, and World War II finally came to an end.

*   *   *   *

To anyone who lived through it, World War II was life-altering—tragically more so for the families of the half million American sons and daughters who lay buried in graveyards around the globe.

On the home front, most of the civilian population had had their lives and careers upended or put on hold as the entire country shifted to a wartime economy that built ships, planes, tanks, and munitions. Now, with the war's end, the nation began the monumental shift back to peacetime. Industries, jobs, and supply chains all had to be turned in new directions.

It was a daunting task, and the War Department was keenly aware that the 12 million men and women in uniform at the end of the war couldn't be released into the economy all at once—there simply weren't enough jobs available.

For some of those military people that meant an added tour of duty in the occupation armies that swarmed across Europe and Japan. For a lucky few it meant a return to college, funded by the GI Bill. For Lee and a large group of fellow soldiers and sailors, it meant a six-month waiting period during which the Armed Forces had to find something for them to do.

To his good fortune, Lee ended up at Camp Pendleton near San Diego, where he was assigned to the ambulance pool—a job that would immediately provide a grand opportunity for his burgeoning entrepreneurial talents.

With so many changes underway coupled with the huge number of people involved, the demobilization process didn't always go smoothly. Overstaffing and lax supervision were commonplace, and Lee immediately encountered both in the form of his commanding officer's laissez-faire management style: if the sailors in the ambulance pool got the job done and stayed out of trouble, he left them alone.

This was all the direction Lee needed. By his second week on the job he had convinced his fellow ambulance drivers to reorganize. Rather than the typical schedule of five days each week, with their shifts rotating between nights and days throughout the month, Lee introduced a new routine: in groups of twos the sailors would take turns working a 48-hour shift—ready at all hours to respond as necessary. The rest of each week they'd have five days off in a row.

This new schedule proved wildly successful, and it allowed Lee ample time to begin a part-time civilian job long before his enlistment ended. Impressively, he also used this time to take advantage of a Navy program in which he earned a high school diploma and, later, a private pilot's license, but far and away the most memorable accomplishment during this period was his short career in the beverage business.

For obvious reasons, alcohol was tightly controlled at Camp Pendleton. For equally obvious reasons, the average sailor or soldier was constantly trying to remedy this situation, but the guard stations at every entrance were quite effective at enforcement. Incoming vehicles and pedestrians were regularly searched for contraband. However (and this proved to be rather significant for Lee's purposes), they never searched emergency vehicles *during* an emergency.

So, striking a delicate balance between product demand and personal risk, Lee would drive the empty ambulance out one guarded exit, proceed to the nearest liquor store, and load up. Then, with the ambulance fully stocked with alcohol, he'd drive to a different guard station, punch the siren, and with lights flashing, re-enter the base at high speed. It was an inspired strategy, and Lee's first business venture thrived for the remainder of his enlistment.

*　　*　　*　　*

Lee had joined the military when most of his contemporaries were still in high school and trained for months with the sure expectation that he was about to be put in harm's way. Certainly, most of his fellow World War II veterans had far more harrowing experiences. Still, this period played a huge role in his life, and, like most of his fellow veterans, Lee was old beyond his years when he returned to civilian life.

By and large the men of his generation were a breed unto themselves. Baptized in the greatest economic collapse the world had ever seen, they came of age serving their country in the most destructive war mankind had ever unleashed.

As a group, they were hard-working, self-reliant, and, much like the movie hero of their day, John Wayne, not overly bothered by emotions. They weren't much bothered by moral uncertainty either. These men had unshakable convictions as to what was right and wrong. Traditional middle-class family values were right, their Country was right, capitalism was right, anything outside those norms was wrong.

It was a moral code that had served for generations. More to the point, it had provided *their* generation with both direction and assurance in a world filled with uncertainty and danger. Yet, within the very purposefulness of that belief system was a rigidity ill-suited to the rapid and monumental changes that lay in the decades ahead, and Lee's generation would find their fixed and unchanging principles chronically out of step with the experiences of future generations.

Still, whatever their faults, one can't help but admire their strengths. In a word, these guys were tough. They had to be. And when World War II was over, the only thing most of them wanted was to settle down to a quiet life of peace and security. For most, those goals began with a steady job, and for Lee, after receiving an honorable discharge from the Navy in early 1946, it meant joining the family's newest business venture ...

CHAPTER 15

Miner's Hardware
(The Original)

Though promisingly situated between Hollywood and Santa Monica, Culver City has never enjoyed the glamor of its more famous neighbors, which meant that throughout most of the 20th century land prices there were relatively cheap.

Most famously, those real estate bargains had attracted the attention of Metro Goldwyn Mayer (MGM) who, during the Roaring Twenties, purchased 160 acres in the middle of town and filled it with soundstages, offices, and the legendary "Back Lot" where movies like *Gone with the Wind, Ben Hur* and a host of musicals were shot.

Less famously (though more importantly for our story) Abe was also attracted to Culver City real estate prices, and in 1944, just a few blocks south of MGM Studios, he and Bee purchased an empty retail building with a large sales floor on the bottom and a small apartment upstairs.[22]

---

22 Today Culver City's population has trebled, MGM is now owned by Sony, and most of the "Back Lot" along with Miner's Hardware original location have all been sold to developers.

It was here, following Lee's unpleasantness with the vice principal in Blythe, that the family took up temporary residence and, after the war (and the closure of the mine) it became the site of Abe's next business venture: retail hardware.

It was an idea that made little sense to Bee or anyone else (when it came to home improvement projects, Abe wasn't exactly a "hands-on" kind of guy). Yet, once again he had recognized a paradigm shift: in the world of retail business, supply would determine success.

Throughout World War II most consumer goods had either been in short supply or not available at all, and Abe figured that with that level of pent-up demand he could sell just about anything. The trick was going to be getting it.

For the next few years Abe worked every connection he had, finagled his way into the offices of wholesalers and manufacturers, and managed to keep Miner's Hardware supplied with merchandise. There were still shortages, but, overall, the store was known for having merchandise no one else seemed able to get.

In one instance (and a story Abe was always proud to tell) he was able to purchase an entire truckload of galvanized buckets and wash tubs. In normal times this would have represented a few years' supply, but throughout the entire war nothing galvanized had been available to consumers—all production had been used by the Navy. So, when the truckload of merchandise arrived in late 1946, Miner's Hardware sold the entire contents in a few days.

*   *   *   *

Miner's Hardware in Culver City, circa 1949. Opened by Abe and Bee in 1946, it closed in 1955 when they tried retirement. Miner's Hardware in Grover Beach—still in operation today—was opened by their sons, Lee and Glenn, in 1956.

From the start, Miner's Hardware was a family business, where everyone lived and worked under the same roof. Glenn was still in high school, so he worked only part-time, but for Lee this marked the beginning of his career, and he was anxious to get to work. He was in luck as far as the work part went, because Miner's Hardware was open every day but Sunday, and 60-hour workweeks were the norm. It was a brutal schedule, though typical for most small businesses at the time (and one Lee would keep well into his middle age).

Pictures from the late 1940s reveal a store that was obviously well-run: clean, organized, and fully stocked. However, by today's standards it was monumentally old school. Everything was priced by hand, and if the products were displayed at all they were generally laid next to one another on waist-high shelves. Flashlight batteries, for example, were sold in bulk from the cardboard box they'd been shipped in. The price of each was marked on the outside of the box and customers grabbed as many they needed.

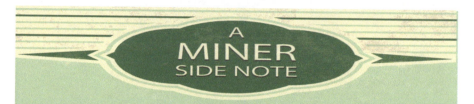

A MINER SIDE NOTE

CULVER CITIZEN NEWSPAPER, AUG. 1947

(An article that reads suspiciously like it was written by Abe Miner.)

Lee Miner, who serves forth nuts, bolts, and garbage cans (when he can get them) to the patrons of the Washington-Sepulveda district, has reached the pinnacle. Anything that happens to him from now on will be in the nature of an anti-climax.

Lee was showing one of his famous Servel Refrigerators to a customer. The shopper studied the box at length, agreed to the obvious advantages of a unit that keeps quiet and doesn't have to shuffle a bunch of machinery around to produce an ice cube, then bought it.

In writing up the sale, Miner asked for the man's name and was given an unpronounceable string of consonants. Curious, he asked the buyer the origin of the name that took two tongues to pronounce.

Believe it or not, Lee Miner, standing in the Miner's Hardware store at 11143 Washington Blvd., had sold a Servel to an Eskimo.

Fully half the items in the store—things like pipefittings, fasteners, and wire—had their prices stored in the Master Price Book, which was kept at the cash register, and had to be looked up for each transaction. At checkout all invoices were added by hand (there were no calculators or computers), and all inventory control was based completely on human memory—"Hey, did we order two of those widgets last week or was it four?"

The products themselves could be even more antiquated. Most paint contained lead and all of it was oil-based, which, besides the toxic fumes, meant brushes and everything else had to be cleaned with paint thinner. Clotheslines were ever popular because nobody owned an automatic clothes dryer, and one of the bestselling items in the store was a trash incinerator—necessary because weekly trash pickup didn't yet exist, so everyone burned their trash in the backyard.

Yet, despite all those ancient products and procedures, Miner's Hardware continued to grow—so much so that only a few years after opening, the store was remodeled, and the inventory expanded to include major appliances.

Like his father, Lee seemed to have a knack for business, and gradually assumed ever greater responsibilities for running the store. By his early 20s he was often in charge as Abe and Bee began taking more time off. However, as good as he was becoming at business, his fame within the immediate family tended more toward the athletic, or at least that's the story his brother told.

Apparently, just before Christmas of 1949 Lee had managed to purchase a large quantity of pogo sticks—the hottest new product on the market and the feature item in the hardware store's seasonal

Toy Department that year. Anxious to promote their sale, Lee quickly became a pogo stick whiz, and would often impress customers as he "pogoed" through the store.

His grand finale was a remarkable three-foot vertical leap out the back door of the store and onto the open tailgate of a waiting pickup truck. It was quite the crowd pleaser until a poorly timed takeoff caused him to miss. Similar to his rattlesnake misadventure he landed in a heap; only this time along with the embarrassment of the moment, he had to deal with the added humiliation of hobbling around on crutches for two weeks with torn ligaments in his ankle.

By 1950 Miner's Hardware had become something of an institution within its hometown of Culver City. It had a solid base of loyal customers, who were driving sales steadily upwards, and it was becoming particularly well known for one of its specialty departments.

Lee, Glenn, Bee, and Abe Miner, Culver City, 1948.

Lee Miner (left) and Wally Lewis in the Sporting Goods Department, 1950
(we'll learn more about Wally in future chapters).

Likely due to the Miner Family's near obsession with hunting and fishing, the Sporting Goods Department had become the largest section within the store. It offered hard-to-find products and advice from people who knew what they were talking about. In fact, it was becoming such an entity unto itself that Abe decided to separate it from the rest of the business and make Sporting Goods a store within a store.

Lee purchased the inventory, paid rent for his portion of the floor space, and began to run the department as his own separate business.

For the next few years the idea worked for everyone as both businesses grew in sales and customer count.

For many of those customers, especially the local sportsmen, Miner's became their store of choice. They made frequent visits for purchases large and small and looked upon the arrival of the newest fishing reel or shotgun as something akin to Christmas morning. These men were serious about their sport, and one fisherman in particular was about to become Lee's most important customer.

CHAPTER 16

The Newtons

His name was James V (Jim) Newton, and he will play many roles as our narrative continues, including, eventually, that of my maternal grandfather, "Grampy." To the rest of the world he was a businessman, a family man, and most especially a lover of people.

He loved being in social groups of every kind; he loved hearing stories; he loved telling stories; he loved being of service; he loved having friends, and they loved him in return. Indeed, when it came to his fellow man, Grampy would become something of a rock star, and at the end, his funeral would fill the biggest church in Culver City, where people were standing shoulder to shoulder in the back of the church and along the aisles because there was nowhere left to sit.

Of course, Grampy played other roles outside family and friends, but never with the same level of engagement. In finance, for example, he paid his bills on time and provided adequately for his family, but beyond the basics he quickly lost interest. His talents lay elsewhere.

* * * *

The Newton family lived just a few blocks south of Miner's Hardware in a sprawling neighborhood of small two-bedroom homes built in the late 1930's. Typical of the time the lots were closely spaced with a small front yard, each sporting a single tree near the street.

It was a neighborhood populated almost entirely by working-class families who took pride in what they had accomplished. The houses were regularly repainted, the lawns regularly mowed, and the ubiquitous rose bushes regularly pruned. Overhead the trees had grown to such a height that their branches formed a giant canopy of green that completely spanned the street, and that, combined with the meticulously cared-for front yards produced an overall effect that bordered on elegance. Altogether, it was a completely satisfactory place to raise a family, and it's unlikely anyone was more pleased to be there than Jim and his wife, Ella Mae (Peggie) Newton.

They had married in a ceremony that remains singularly unusual (and singularly out of character for Peggie). With no money for a formal wedding, they had planned a simple justice of the peace ceremony at City Hall, until Jim (acting completely *in* character) intervened.

It was the fall of 1930, and in a clever promotion for the upcoming Los Angeles County Fair, the local radio station was running a contest wherein some lucky young couple would be married for free. The catch was that the ceremony had to take place in an airplane that would be circling the fairgrounds.

How they won the contest and (more to the point) how Jim ever talked Peggie into entering the contest remains a family mystery, but on September 24, 1930, they boarded an eight-passenger Fairchild airplane complete with pilot, minister, and witnesses. Twenty minutes later they landed, and the local newspaper ran a picture of the new Mr. and Mrs. J.V. Newton, with the plane in the background.

By almost any calculation it was a marriage that shouldn't have worked. More so even than Abe and Bee, Jim and Peggie each saw the world through different lenses. Jim was the classic Irishman—devoutly Catholic, gregarious, quick to anger and quicker to forgive, the type of man who never met a stranger. Peggie was of mostly German descent and had the demeanor of a Prussian general to prove it. She was disciplined, reserved, and a closet atheist who believed that if justice ever prevailed, it did so only by personal intervention. Yet, despite these monumental differences, they shared a handful of deeply held values.

They had both come from poor families and desperate circumstances. Jim, who grew up in Detroit, had been orphaned at age 15 and left to fend for himself. Peggie's family had remained more or less intact, but that hardly mattered. Her mother was uncaring and her stepfather cruel and abusive.

Jim and Peggie Newton (center left) and wedding party.

For Jim and Peggie together, it's doubtful they possessed more than a handful of happy childhood memories, and that ugly fact would produce in them a fervent commitment to create a better future. For the rest of their lives, nothing—least of all themselves—was more important than their children and grandchildren.

In quick succession they had four daughters, though, just as tragically as in the Miner Family, only two survived: Joanie, born in 1931, and Kathie, born in 1940. Separated by age and personality, the girls were never close, but each had fond memories of their respective childhoods, and they were both especially close to their father.

As his daughters were growing up, Jim worked a number of different jobs, including a stint at Hughes Aircraft during World War II where he worked on the assembly line of one of the more unusual projects of the war. Conceived in 1942, when the German U-Boat threat in the Atlantic was at its peak, the idea was to build an aircraft large enough to *fly* troops and supplies directly to England rather than send them by ship.

The "solution" was the Hughes H-4 Hercules, the biggest plane ever built (until 1988) and also one of the most problematic. Beset by a host of technical problems the project was nearly scrapped altogether when the War Department (in a noteworthy display of bureaucratic schizophrenia) first funded the project, then denied it the aluminum necessary to construct it.

Undeterred, Howard Hughes and his team of engineers turned to a recently developed product called *Duramold* (basically a very strong and lightweight version of plywood) and eventually completed a single prototype two years after the war had ended. Dubbed the *Spruce Goose*, the plane made a single 26-second flight and never flew again.

Today it resides in the Evergreen Aviation and Space Museum— the pride of their collection.

The Spruce Goose (H-4 Hercules) in Long Beach, November 2, 1947. Note the people standing on the wing, which is longer than a football field and 96 feet longer than the wingspan of a 747. (Courtesy of the Welcome Home, Howard Digital Collection, UNLV University Libraries Special Collections.)

* * * *

After the war Jim took a position with the *Los Angeles Times* and settled into a career that would last the rest of his life. As jobs went, this one was rare. He and a small group of fellow independent contractors (called "dealers") each owned the distribution rights for a specific area of Southern California where the *Los Angeles Times* was delivered. Jim's area included portions of Culver City and Santa Monica, where he and his crew of carriers were responsible for delivering several thousand papers to residences and business each day.

Accomplishing this task meant their workday began at 2 a.m. when the papers started arriving at their regional distribution points—in Jim's case, a small warehouse that he shared with another dealer.

It was a tough, dirty job and the men Jim hired as carriers looked the part. (From my impressionable boyhood perspective—which we'll get to in chapter 24—I first assumed they were all former pirates.)

Each morning they arrived at work unshaven, un-bathed, dressed in old dirty clothes, and, judging from the prevalence of missing teeth, a general disregard for dental hygiene. As a group they were mostly social misfits who for various reasons couldn't keep a regular job, although notably mixed in were usually one or two young go-getters who needed a temporary second income.

Altogether they were an unusual mix of humanity from every age group and often headed in opposite directions on the economic ladder. Yet despite their differences, they all shared three basic traits: they weren't afraid of hard work; they needed a job bad enough to get up and go to work in the middle of the night; and they all quit the moment their circumstances improved.

In sum, the newspaper delivery business demanded a work schedule that was hard to like, even on the good days. On the bad days, when carriers called in sick or quit without notice, or the papers arrived late, or it rained unexpectedly, everything would suddenly become much worse. On those days Jim might work 12 hours straight, and when carriers were in short supply the bad days could sometimes go on for weeks.

Fortunately, the operation worked most of the time. Jim typically had one or two days off each week, and through a reciprocal agreement with a fellow dealer, he managed to get a few weeks of vacation every year, but the demands of the job never varied: customers wanted their papers delivered every morning of every single day and they wanted them early.

Generally speaking, it proved to be a satisfactory career. The Newtons were never rich—their home was the only significant asset they ever owned—yet they managed to live a solid middle-class lifestyle. Their daughters both went to college, the family was able to take modest vacations, and Jim even had enough extra time to pursue his one passion: fishing.

When it came to fishing, Jim wasn't particular. On the ocean, by a stream, or at a lake—it didn't seem to matter whether he even *caught* fish. If he was away from work, with one or two of his buddies, and a line was in the water, life was as good as it could get. Naturally, having the right equipment was part of the experience, and Jim was as enthusiastic about fishing gear as any man who ever lived. So, when the hardware store down the street began carrying fishing rods, reels, and all the assorted tackle to go with them, it didn't take him long to check the place out.

Thrilled with the new Sporting Goods Department, Jim was soon on a first-name basis with the entire Miner Family. More particularly, he was especially impressed with the oldest son, Lee. In him, Jim saw a promising young man who came from a solid family, was hardworking, eager to succeed, and loved fishing almost as much as he did.

Of course, none of this would have mattered if it hadn't been for one very important detail: residing within the Newton household at this time was Jim's 20-year-old daughter, Joanie.

Just beginning her sophomore year in college, she was intelligent, attractive, and by Jim's estimation, not enjoying much of a social life at school, which presumably is what prompted him to bring her along on one of his trips to Miner's Hardware.

Her appearance made quite the impression on Lee, and much to the surprise of both the Newton and Miner families, quickly led to a string of unforeseen consequences which will soon begin to reverberate through the remainder of our story. But before getting to all that, we should first turn our attention towards the young lady in question.

CHAPTER 17

Joanie

S he was born Myrtle Joan Newton—a first name that, curiously, her parents seemed not particularly fond of because it was almost immediately dropped in favor of Joanie. She grew up a good Catholic girl—a faith she remained committed to throughout her life. She attended Catholic grammar school, an all-girls Catholic high school, and in the fall of 1950 entered Mount Saint Mary's, an all-girls Catholic university.

It was a sheltered education, to be sure. Yet, despite its strict moral framework and lack of gender diversity, Joanie did manage to meet a sprinkling of both Protestants and boys.

The neighborhood in which she grew up was full of young families with children, and that, coupled with her parents' involvement in numerous social clubs, provided a ready source of friends outside school. However, what was likely her most significant experience with a larger world happened at Paradise Cove.

As the name implies, Paradise Cove occupies a particularly beautiful setting tucked into the California coastline about 25 miles north of Culver City. It was here, in the summers following World War II (the late 1940s, when Joanie was a teenager), that the Newton family arrived each summer with their small travel trailer for a two-week vacation. It was an annual adventure that marked a special time and place, and between the beach, family activities, and most especially a small group of fellow teenagers who arrived under similar circumstances, Joanie would remember those summer vacations as the best time in her life.

Most of those teenagers would go on to lives and careers that were relatively traditional, but at least two were destined for Hollywood. One of the boys became a moderately successful director, and one of the girls, who was at Paradise Cove for only a single summer, became

Joanie Newton, second from left, with friends at Paradise Cove, 1948.

the legendary actress, Elizabeth Taylor. Yet, in spite of the different directions their lives would all take, it's surprisingly easy to see the excitement of this particular period, because in the summer of 1948 a small group of them got together to make a movie.

This notable piece of cinematography was a cleverly conceived melodrama involving heroes, villains, illegal drugs, and a female lead with the catchy name of Mary Wanna. As a work of art their movie is unlikely ever to be confused with the *Maltese Falcon, Key Largo*, or any of the film noir classics, but it obviously aspired to that genre. Granted, at only 10 minutes duration, *Mary Wanna* lacked the scope of its more famous rivals. Indeed, it lacked even a soundtrack, but its star instantly turned the film into the most memorable movie ever made …according to her three children.

So, let us fast-forward about 40 years from our story's current timeline. It's the late 1980s and Joanie, who is nearly 60 years old by now, has just received an unexpected package in the mail from her old (director) friend.

Inside the box is a single videotape accompanied by a note explaining that the sender had recently found the original 8mm film, *Mary Wanna*—thought by all to have been lost forever. The enclosed copy was a gift for the star of the movie, Joan Newton—the very same Joan Newton who, only three years after her cinematic debut, would become my mother.

Judging by her reaction, that tape may have been the most exciting and unexpected gift Mom ever received. At least that's what it sounded like when she called me at work and asked if I could stop by early the next morning in order to see an old movie.

I had no idea what I was in for …

Before pressing the play button, Mom quickly explained the film's origin and that she and her friends had together written, starred, directed, and filmed the video I was about to see. The opening credits silently rolled by in grainy black and white, and then without warning, the star and femme fatale of *Mary Wanna* made her dramatic entrance.

It was shocking, and by this, I mean that I immediately went into shock, which by itself is highly unusual. Normally in situations of extreme discomfort I opt for simple denial—a strategy I've generally found to be both comforting and effective. Unfortunately, the evidence before me was simply too overwhelming to allow that choice. Shock would have to do, and I remained in that state throughout the first showing.

No doubt there is a normal and correct reaction to watching one's 18-year-old future mother (who was absolutely gorgeous) vamp across the screen in high heels, a tight skirt, and an even tighter blouse, but I still have no idea what that might be. I did, however, immediately begin to wonder how much long-term therapy I was likely to require.

Still enthralled by what she was seeing, Mom played the movie again, this time adding a behind-the-scenes commentary on the making of the film along with details about the cast. It was easy to see why *Mary Wanna* was so important to her: a small company of friends, a shared purpose, and all of them so full of life and promise that even after all these years, the enthusiasm and force of their youth practically jumped off the screen.

As the movie came to an end for the second time, neither Mom nor I spoke—each of us absorbed in our own thoughts. After all those many years, Mom must surely have been looking back at lost loves, forgotten friends, and paths not taken.

On my side, trying to incorporate *Mary Wanna* within my framework of "Mom" was proving impossible. How could the 18-year-old vixen on the screen be the nearly 60-year-old woman sitting next to me?

Of course, the almost forty years separating those two women did hint at some of my confusion, but only part. The larger problem, I finally realized, was that there was still much I didn't know about my own mother. What other secrets did she hold? What else about her did I not understand?

"A great many things," I would eventually conclude.

Sadly, even today much of Mom remains a conundrum; however, there were two important pieces of her puzzle that would fall into place after her death. So, in the interest of sparing the Gentle Reader decades of unnecessary confusion, our narrative will remain in "Back to the Future" mode for the remainder of this chapter.

*   *   *   *

More than 20 years after first seeing *Mary Wanna* (and 15 years after Mom's death), I arrived at the Getty Museum on a clear and crisp morning in the spring of 2011. One of the great museums of the world, it sits high atop the hills of Santa Monica, where stunning views of the Pacific Ocean, magnificent architecture, and a world-class art collection all combine in a brilliant example of the whole becoming greater than the sum of its parts. But, as superlative as The Getty remains, the real reason for my being there was to spend time with my uncle Al for two important reasons: first, at age 77 he had recently become a widower, when his wife, Aunt Kathie (Mom's only sister), had died suddenly and unexpectedly from a pulmonary embolism; and second, because he was still breathing.

I realize this last condition isn't much of a standard; however, I was quickly running out of relatives. Indeed, with the passing of Aunt Kathie, I was now the oldest surviving member of our immediate family, which (to borrow my brother's favorite metaphor) meant that I was no longer "on deck." It was my "up" and I was now at the plate swinging away. So, even though Al was my uncle only by marriage,

A MINER SIDE NOTE

AL ... MY RETIREMENT HERO

An electrical engineer by trade, Al was active physically and mentally throughout his career, and when he retired at age 65 he was determined to stay that way.

So, shortly before his last day at work, he purchased and began reading *The Story of Civilization* by Will and Ariel Durant—an 11-volume set that runs to nearly 10,000 pages!

At the same time Al enrolled in sailing classes at nearby Marina del Rey, where he learned how to captain a 26-foot Catalina sailboat.

Later, with those self-imposed tasks completed, Al began a new set of challenges—a strategy he maintained for the rest of his life.

and we didn't share a single hereditary gene, I still had a deep and irrational appreciation for his continued earthly presence.

He was also one of the most kind-hearted and intellectually curious men I'd ever known, and we spent a delightful day together wandering the galleries and catching up on each other's lives: first over an early lunch and later during afternoon tea.

Al and I had much to discuss, but as so often occurs, the most interesting and thought-provoking conversation of the day happened quite by accident as we sat admiring the view from the dining room's many windows.

Al, who had lived in the area most of his adult life, began pointing out some of the landmarks—Santa Monica, downtown L.A., Bel Air, etc.—when he directed my attention northward across the canyon. There atop the adjacent mountaintop was a cluster of stately buildings, surrounded by a manicured landscape and a small forest of trees. Pointing to the complex and noting its commanding view of the coastline, Al mentioned we were looking at Mount Saint Mary's College.

It was Mom's alma mater—a place I'd heard her mention many times but had never before seen and, until now, had no idea how resplendent the campus actually was. It looked like something out of *Camelot*, and I immediately began to wonder what it must have been like when Mom was a student there so many years ago.

She had graduated valedictorian of her high school class, which would have opened doors to almost every college in the nation (or at least the ones that accepted women). Apparently, Mount Saint Mary's was her first choice.

It was Catholic (naturally), had an excellent academic reputation, was within commuting distance from her parents' home in Culver City, and, though Mom had never mentioned this part, was among the most beautiful campuses on the planet. For the first time, I started connecting the dots.

Mom had entered college in 1950, when only 8% of women went on to higher education. Always a straight 'A' student, she would have relished being part of the rarefied scholastic and social environment of university life—a star competitor in a field of play that mattered most to her. Then, near the beginning of her sophomore year, she went on her first date with Lee Miner. Six weeks later he proposed.

A MINER SIDE NOTE

THE WEIRDNESS OF TIME

While Al and I were slowly enjoying our pot of tea and trying to work out the details of Mom's college experience, a separate portion of my brain (which often plays quietly by itself with numbers) suddenly interrupted with a startling observation: *exactly* 60 years had passed—perhaps to the day—when Mom had found her life at a crossroads on the very college campus Al and I were admiring over tea.

At that moment the universe seemed to lose its cohesion and I was staring across space and time. Obviously, the decision she was agonizing over would be of some consequence to her, but it was going to mean *everything* to me.

Surely Mom would have recognized her life was at a crossroads, and, as I continued to stare at the campus, it was easy to imagine her walking alone through the forested landscape or sitting quietly on a bench gazing out over the Pacific and searching for answers. Likely for the first time in her life she would have found herself caught in the age-old paradox of the heart feeling things the mind cannot understand. Before her were an almost infinite series of what-ifs, all of which coalesced into a choice between two radically different futures ...

It must have been delicious agony.

To the complete surprise of family and friends, Mom accepted and dropped out of college. In December of 1951, Lee and Joanie were married. (I arrived the following August.)

*   *   *   *

For reasons owing entirely to my fondness for personal existence, I've always appreciated Mom and Dad's union, even though it never made much sense to me. Fundamentally, Mom was the dutiful Catholic daughter, outgoing like her father, and blessed with her mother's keen intellect. Dad, on the other hand, was the rebel-atheist, no-time-for-school introvert.

I suppose one could argue they were each following in their parents' footsteps, whose prescription for mate selection appeared to be: *find your opposite and hope for the best.*

Not a particularly promising formula, to be sure. And, though it had apparently worked in previous generations, Mom and Dad never seemed to enjoy the same level of success. Then again, it didn't prove entirely fatal to their marriage either. Regardless, there had always remained for me the basic question as to why on earth Mom ever agreed to marry Dad in the first place.

Quite remarkably the (obvious) answer to that question lay buried in the bottom of a drawer, where it wouldn't be discovered until long after they were both gone …

In early 2000, my sister and brother, Kitty and Steve, flew home for Grammie's funeral (Peggie Newton, our maternal grandmother). The service was a small affair, attended only by immediate family, and afterwards the three of us gathered together to look through our grandmother's few remaining possessions. We were each of us in our 40s by now and, because most of our family members had proven to be unusually short-lived, the three of us had been through this unwanted ritual many times before.

In Grammie's case, however, most of the work had already been done. Some 20 years previously, after Grampy's death, Grammie had sold the family home in Culver City and moved north to a much smaller house located a few miles from her oldest daughter (our mom). Later, as Grammie's health and mental capacity declined, she moved through a series of ever smaller retirement and care facilities, which meant that, after searching through a couple of drawers and cupboards, we quickly gathered together her few remaining personal effects.

They fit into a single cardboard box and contained a handful of family pictures, a few carefully clipped newspaper articles, an assortment of old greeting cards and letters, and some trinkets from long-ago vacations.

The last and most valuable treasures of an entire lifetime, they had been rendered awkwardly and uncomfortably inert. Like stories that contained only an opening sentence, each trinket was now forever severed from the only person who could give it context and meaning.

Uneasily, we began the process of passing collective judgment on what would be kept, who would do the keeping, and what would be cast away forever, when Kitty made a completely unexpected discovery: a heretofore unnoticed envelope addressed in careful penmanship to Mr. and Mrs. J.V. Newton.

Inside was a handwritten letter from our then newlywed mother, dated December 3, 1951. It was an unanticipated find, and we were more than curious. Why had Grammie kept a letter for nearly 50 years? Had Mom known it still existed? … Steve and I listened intently as Kitty began to read its contents.

The stationery boldly proclaimed *El Rancho Barstow Hotel*, which, we were about to learn, was where Mom and Dad had spent the first night of their honeymoon. Apparently, Mom awoke early the next morning and, with our future dad still asleep, wrote home for the first time as Mrs. Miner.

The style was clear, hopeful, and altogether exactly the sort of letter a deliriously happy new bride might produce.

Unfortunately, despite the letter's heartfelt theme of familial gratitude, I'm afraid neither Steve nor I proved up to the task of appreciating it during that first reading. At least that was Kitty's frustrated conclusion when, about halfway through the letter, both her brothers burst out laughing as she read the part where, in Mom's own words, "Last night we knelt down together to ask God to bless us and our marriage."

Now, it's not that Steve and I are *completely* irreverent, but, knowing our father as we did, we both had a strong suspicion of what might have motivated him to get on his knees and begin praying at that moment; and neither of us believed it was spiritual fulfillment.

The fact was that Dad, who had never believed in a higher power, somehow managed to convince our devoutly Catholic (future) mother into marrying him, which all but guaranteed that their relationship had yet to be consummated. Ergo, by the time these newlyweds finally arrived at El Rancho Barstow, Dad would have been willing to do almost anything to change the status quo.

Honestly, the more Steve and I considered the circumstance, the funnier it became—especially because, having been raised Catholic ourselves, we had a fairly accurate idea of what our poor, hapless, soon-to-be father would have been forced to endure in order to marry a good Catholic girl like Mom: meetings with the priest; hours of religious instruction; and signed agreements to raise the children Catholic.

To all this, add the actual wedding ceremony (brutally long even by Catholic standards). Next, the reception, and, finally, a two-hour drive before finally arriving at El Rancho Barstow. Well, one can only imagine our father's state of mind when, at the end of all his suffering and anticipation, his new bride wanted to pray.

Actually, Steve and I were completely confident we knew *exactly* what state of mind Dad would have been in, and it was this combined understanding which prompted our spontaneous, unrehearsed, and (we felt) brilliant rendition of our father's likely response to Mom's idea about praying ...

You want to pray first?

Are you shitting m—?

No, wait. Of course, I'd like to pray!

What would you like me to say?

Are we going to do an animal sacrifice next?

I saw a dog outside … Hold on, I'll go get it!

I must say that Steve and I both thought this imagined scene was rather funny. Who am I kidding? We thought it was hysterical, and, gasping for breath in between tears of laughter, we had just begun to discuss between ourselves the differences between praying versus begging and whether, given the circumstances, our 24-year-old father would have either known or cared.

Lamentably, it was just at this point in our impromptu comedy routine that the two of us realized we were in danger of losing our single audience member. Frankly, we were in danger—period. Kitty was starting to use words like "incorrigible" and "adolescent" and, in an eerie and scary sort of way, had suddenly begun to look and sound just like our own mother. Steve and I knew that look, we knew that tone of voice, and we knew we were just seconds from having to stand in the corner or go to our room if we didn't start to behave.

It was a close thing. Kitty paused for effect, glanced up at each of her much taller but at the moment completely intimidated brothers, and asked, "Are you done?"

Apparently, we were. With supreme effort Steve and I tried to look remorseful, even if we both knew Kitty wouldn't buy it. Nevertheless, we did manage to stop laughing, and, by not daring to look at one another, succeeded in remaining quiet for the remainder of the reading …

More than two decades have now passed since that long-ago afternoon when the three of us first read Mom's letter, and, as strange as this must sound, it remains the single best memory I have of my original family. Even with Steve's and my initial and irreverent behavior, it was an affirming moment of trust and appreciation between siblings, along with the most unexpected discovery that Mom and Dad had once been young, full of life, and, to our great surprise, deeply in love. Suddenly, both our parents appeared far more multidimensional than we'd ever given them credit for.

At some intellectual level we all knew Mom and Dad must have been innocent young newlyweds at one time. There was even some vague (and I think the word I'm looking for here might be "antiseptic") realization that, having delivered the three of us, Mom must also have been sexually active on at least three occasions. However, there's a big difference between holding a deliberately unexamined fact like that in one's head versus holding an actual letter in one's hand that alludes to those sorts of things.

When it comes to our parents, we all tend to be myopic, and this seems to be particularly true of mothers. Isn't Mom's real purpose to take care of us (children)? How could she have a life that didn't center itself upon that supremely important task?

It's delusional thinking, to be sure, and yet so powerfully imprinted in our childhood consciousness that, even as adults, most of us find it difficult to recognize and dismiss such a pleasant fantasy.

At least that's my excuse.

Joanie and Lee Miner, 1951.

In any case, we're going to leave the task of Mom's proper job description to others, and, instead, return to the chronological thread of our story, where it's still the middle of the 20th century and where most of our characters are about to find their lives moving in surprisingly new directions.

CHAPTER 18

The Road to Alaska

By mid-1954 the days of Miner's Hardware in Culver City were coming to an end. In part this was due to Lee and Glenn—both had recently married and were pursuing career paths outside the family business—but the bigger reason had to do with Abe. With a consistency that must have sorely tested Bee's patience, Abe's attention span with any business would never exceed eight years, and in his mind the hardware store had reached its expiration date.

There was, however, something different about this time. After closing down the hardware store, instead of immediately searching for a new venture, Abe and Bee decided to try retirement.

The attempt would soon fail—neither of them could ever sit still for long—but they did at least put some thought into making it work.

After purchasing a new pickup truck, Abe hired a carpenter to build a prototype of today's mini-camper—complete with bed, portable stove, fishing gear, and a watertight metal covering. Though basic to the point of being primitive it was luxurious compared to tent camping, and Bee provisioned it with everything necessary for an extended journey.

Spring of 1955 saw them heading slowly north through the Pacific Northwest and into Canada, where they arrived at the beginning of what was then one of the wonders of the world: the Alcan Highway.

Built during the early days of World War II by the Army Corps of Engineers it connected the continental U.S. with Alaska for the first time via a 1,700-mile road that crossed the length of British Columbia. Narrow, unpaved, often impassable during the winter, and subject to washouts all the rest of the year, it nevertheless represented a stunning achievement.

Bee, fishing along the Alcan Highway, 1955.

Just three months after Pearl Harbor, 10,000 men—a third of whom were soldiers of the newly formed African American regiments—began construction in March of 1942, and completed the project in the impossibly short time of nine months. (Today it takes an average of one year to construct a *single* interstate highway bridge.)

The Alcan Highway was exactly the kind of adventure that suited them both, and for the entire summer Abe and Bee wandered along that gravel roadway visiting towns, villages, and outposts. They fished the rivers and lakes, were awed by magnificent vistas, and camped wherever they wanted, until finally reaching the end of the road at Anchorage.

Fall had arrived and, with the days quickly getting shorter and colder, they needed to head back south. Considering briefly a return journey over the miles and miles of bone-jarring gravel road they'd just traveled, Abe and Bee opted instead for the ferry. With a view cabin and their truck safely stored below deck, they cruised the Inside Passage—a string of (mostly) protected waterways that meander down the coast of Southeast Alaska and British Columbia. A few days later they arrived at the ferry terminal in Bellingham, Washington.

It was the trip of a lifetime and marked the longest vacation they would ever take. It also marked the end of their entire retirement plan—an oversight that was about to change the lives of generations.

Heading generally south—with the vague intention of returning to Culver City—Abe and Bee, instead, stopped at Shell Beach. One of several small towns clustered on the Central Coast of California, it was sparsely populated, breathtakingly beautiful, and had long been their favorite vacation destination.

Here they rented a small home and Abe began looking for something to do. He would eventually start several more businesses, but the opportunity that almost immediately presented itself was a small hardware store for sale in Grover Beach.[23] Convinced it was an opportunity, he presented the deal to his sons and, for the first

23 In 1982 Grover City would change its name to Grover Beach. For simplicity, Grover Beach is used throughout this book.

and only time in his life, assumed a supporting role. Abe and Bee never owned any part of what was soon to become the new Miner's Hardware. Instead, they provided most of the financing, and helped during the transition, when, in early 1956, Lee and Glenn quit their jobs in LA and moved their very young families to a new world.

CHAPTER 19

The '50s

J oanie was 19 years old when the 1950s arrived—a decade that
would have proven difficult for just about anyone—particularly if
you happened to be young, inexperienced, and female.

Certainly, any historical period can be problematic—the Roaring
20s, the Great Depression of the '30s, the Counterculture of the 60's,
and so on—but for just plain weirdness nothing beats the self-inflicted
psychosis of the 1950s when society's myth of the "ideal woman"
crashed full speed into the emerging Women's Movement.

For Joanie it would be a (not always welcome) first-person
experience of a world sent hurtling in directions unimagined by
previous generations. Moreover, as a soon-to-be wife and mother, she
was about to find herself in just the right place, at just the right time,
and at just the right age to experience the full force of the cultural
earthquake that the decade was about to unleash.

*   *   *   *

Unless you actually lived through the 1950s or have a degree in
history, it's unlikely the poor-quality photograph and caption shown

below will provide much insight into the world Mom found herself confronting throughout her 20s.

Incredibly, (and to the gentle reader's good fortune), our narrator *did* live through most of the 1950s and *does* have a degree in history. It would therefore seem remiss not to provide a few insightful paragraphs as to just how strange and difficult this period really was.

To begin, the 1950s ushered in a period of social confusion unprecedented in American history. Less than five years had passed since the end of World War II, and, while the general population may have longed to return to the simpler times of the past, too many genies had been let out of the bottle.

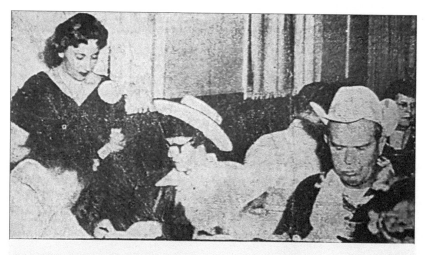

ENCHILADA DINNER—Women's Club candidate for honorary mayor, Mrs. Leland Miner, watches over patrons at an enchilada dinner while Charlie Warner with his mouth full of Spanish food seems interested in the work at hand. Mrs. Warner seems a little undecided as to just how much of this Spanish food is good for one on a diet.—Press photo.

A generation before, most Americans had never left the farm. Now hundreds of thousands of GIs had seen the world. Perhaps an even greater catalyst for change came from the unintended consequences of manpower shortages caused by the war. From 1941-1945 vast numbers of women rose to the challenge and entered the workforce. They built fighter planes, ran locomotives, and launched ships. That first taste of equality and opportunity couldn't be forgotten. A similar awakening came to those minorities who both served in the military and on the home front.

The geopolitical stage was more confusing still as old empires lay in ruins and new empires were forged, including the U.S.'s new nuclear-armed adversary, the Soviet Union.

In combination, these changing paradigms would shatter the status quo and lead to the Cold War, the women's movement, the civil rights movement, Vietnam, and more—but not quite yet.

America's first panicked response was a spasm of traditionalism as forces within society tried desperately to return to the past, and nowhere was this tug-of-war more evident than in the myth of the "ideal woman."

According to traditionalists, women were expected to be wives and mothers. Careers in teaching, nursing, and secretarial work were (barely) acceptable, but those jobs were never allowed to interfere with a husband's career, nor did they provide relief from a woman's ongoing maternal and domestic responsibilities.

Curiously, this absurd recipe for cultural mental illness was best displayed by advertisers. In what later generations would consider a comedic parody, women of the fifties were regularly portrayed spending their days joyfully ironing clothes, cleaning ovens, and serving sumptuous dinners to their successful husbands and adoring children.

The underlying truth—that most women found this stereotype both impossible to maintain and deeply unfulfilling—had yet to be acknowledged, let alone confronted, and it was this irrational jumble of cultural clashes and social repression that awaited Mom as a 20-year-old bride in late 1951.

Advertisement in Good Housekeeping *magazine, circa 1955.*

Look again at the picture and caption on page 132 and a few of the 1950s cultural biases start to become apparent.

Mom was playing by the rules in terms of appearance, even while breaking the rules as she ran for mayor. She lost, of course (women didn't belong in politics in the '50s), but the more revealing prejudices lies within the caption itself: in the 1950s, married women were an extension of their husbands, and neither Mrs. Leland Miner nor Mrs. Warner were allowed a first name.

It's hard to overstate how socially rigid and male-centric American society was in the early 1950s, and this was especially true in rural areas such as the Central Coast of California, where Mom found herself living as a new bride and mother.[24] Nevertheless, she was bright, enthusiastic, and determined to achieve more than the role society had reserved for her. She just had no idea how difficult it was going to be...

---

24 The Central Coast of California was also extremely white—the first African American family wouldn't arrive until the mid-1960s. Until then the only racial diversity that existed were a few Japanese American families—all of whom had been sent to internment camps during World War II by the U.S. government.

CHAPTER 20

Careers and Compromise

When Mom walked down the aisle in 1951 to become Mrs. Miner, she was just 20 years old. As was typical of that period, she moved directly from her parents' house into an apartment with her new husband. I arrived eight and a half months later, and my sister 18 months after that in 1954.

The year 1956 saw our little family move to the rural Central Coast, and the opening of Miner's Hardware. The next year my brother was born.

By age 26, Mom was "living the dream." She had three small children, a husband with a successful business, and that quintessential symbol of middle-class accomplishment: a brand-new house (with a brand-new mortgage to go with it).

By every measurement society held dear, Mom was triumphant, and I have no doubt she was excited and proud of her life up to this point, but there was a problem looming in her immediate future. Like generations of women before her, society expected Mom to forsake whatever career aspirations she might have in favor of childcare and housework. To Mom, that version of the future would have looked like a living Hell.

She desperately needed a plan, and, in one of the few lucky breaks she ever got, there turned out to be a nearby solution.

Despite the Central Coast's isolation, there existed something of a cultural oasis just 20 miles north—San Luis Obispo. Originally part of a string of Spanish Missions stretching from San Diego to San Francisco, San Luis Obispo was the intellectual, social, and economic center of the county, and, most importantly for Mom's purposes, the home of Cal Poly State University.

Here she would return to college and become a teacher.

It was never revealed how Mom managed to sell the idea to Dad, but to his credit he agreed, knowing full well the financial burden it would create while she went back to school. Unfortunately, that was as far as his tradition-bound sensibilities were able to stretch. He was and would remain a product of his times, which meant that children and household duties would continue to be Mom's sole responsibility.

This arrangement eventually proved unworkable—and lead to a cascade of unhappy consequences—but it sufficed for a time. Mom still had youth and determination on her side, and that combination, along with a keen intellect, was all she needed to succeed in academia. She entered Cal Poly in 1958 and became the first person in her family to earn a college diploma. She then went on to earn her teaching credential in 1961 and later earned a Master's in Education, graduating *summa cum laude* in 1964.

It was an impressive accomplishment under any conditions, but when one adds raising three young children, completing her student

EL RANCHO BARSTOW HOTEL

My early arrival was forever unsettling to Mom and throughout my childhood she would occasionally mention that I had been conceived on her wedding night. Until about age 12, I had no idea what she was talking about (I went to Catholic Grammar School). After that the horrorstruck look on my face soon put an end to any conversation that contained the words "Mom" and "conception" in the same paragraph.

Fast forward some four decades later (shortly after Mom's Wedding Night Letter to her parents had been discovered—see page 121) when I would find myself on a road trip with my nephews (then, ages 10 through 14) that followed Route 66 right through Barstow.

A desert town that bears an uncanny resemblance to Blythe, Barstow is just the sort of place that inspires motorists to speed right on by—but not our little group. Aware of Mom's letter, the boys were nearly as eager to find the El Rancho Barstow Hotel as I was.

It was a weirdly amusing pilgrimage for all concerned, but what still makes me smile about this adventure is imagining Mom's reaction to our visit.

Left to right: Matt, Jake, James, Mike (the author) and Tom.

teaching, and working as a part-time substitute whenever possible—all while maintaining an A average—it becomes downright stunning.

Meanwhile, Dad was forging ahead with his own career. The first two years at Miner's Hardware were a struggle. The inventory was small, sales were slow, and competitors were numerous. Looking at the demographics, no one would have bet on the store's survival, but then, no one could have known how completely determined Lee and Glenn were to succeed. Everything they owned, together with a loan equivalent to several years of their combined annual salary, was riding on the success of Miner's Hardware. They *had* to make it work.

Being the businesses' only employees, they both worked 10-hour days, six days a week. (Like all businesses at that time, the store was closed on Sundays.) It was meager pay as well, because any extra profits were needed to increase inventory and pay down their loan.

Slowly, Miner's Hardware began to prosper. By year three they hired their first employee, Wally Lewis.[25] Business continued to improve, more employees were added, and Dad began spending a portion of his time outside the hardware store.

Through a loophole in the law (and with almost no experience) Dad became a general building contractor. Then, with license in hand and a highly leveraged loan from the bank, he built and sold several homes by working nights and Sundays along with trading materials from the hardware store with local subcontractors for their labor. He dabbled in other ventures as well: starting a small escrow company, and, surprisingly, owning an airplane.

---

25 The same Wally Lewis from the sporting goods department in Culver City. He will appear again in some detail in Chapter 43 "Other Voices."

A MINER SIDE NOTE

OCEANO AIRPORT DEJA VUE

Dad's plane, which he owned with a friend, was a bright red Stinson taildragger (similar to the picture shown), and in 1959, when I was six years-old, he took me for a ride. The takeoff was thrilling, but as soon as we got over the ocean (which happens almost immediately when departing the Oceano Airport) I was terrified—if the plane went down, I'd drown.

Some 25 years later I had my own pilot's license and was eager to take our five-year-old daughter, Amy, on her first airplane ride. Departing from the same airport, as soon as we got over the ocean Amy anxiously turned to me and asked, "How soon are we coming back?"

From the mid-50s to the mid-60s Mom and Dad were about as busy as it was possible for two people to be. For both of them a 60-hour workweek was typical, but if Dad was building a house or Mom was taking a night class, it could easily stretch to 70 hours and drag on for months.

They checked off accomplishments one after another, and by age 35 their economic success alone exceeded the average of most lifetimes.

Their respective careers were thriving, the house they lived in was lovely, and they had three healthy and growing children. Few couples could boast a brighter looking future.

But all that achievement came with sacrifices. In their single-minded drive for success, Mom and Dad were a constant blur of activity, with little time for anything else.

Even the house we lived in became something of a blur, because (owing to Dad's investment strategy) almost every year he sold the house we called home and moved us all into the newest house he'd just built. By the sixth grade I had lived in seven different houses and attended five different schools. Kitty and Steve had similar experiences. As children we never knew the neighbors.

But, as disconnected as our childhood often felt at home, an entirely different experience awaited us whenever we visited our two sets of grandparents. In our young lives, they were the rocks of our world—solid, unchanging, and available. They were always at home. It was always the *same* home, and, as we shall see, 75 percent of them believed that being a grandparent was the most important job in the world.

CHAPTER 21

Abe

(The Outlier ... Again)

Oddly enough, my earliest memory of my four remarkable grandparents begins with Abe. I was almost 4 years old; it was early 1956; and my entire extended family—sister, parents, grandparents, and a single aunt, and uncle—all lived in Culver City, California. It was here Mom and Dad met, my sister and I were born, and I first went to school. It was called nursery school—a very grown-up-sounding name in my young mind—and it was made of bricks. I attended regularly, the teacher was nice, and on this particular day (for reasons that must have included dire necessity), Abe had been tasked with driving me there.

This job was generally reserved for Mom, who always followed a specific and comforting routine: we arrived at the nursery school; she held my hand as we walked into the classroom; once there she waited patiently until I began to engage with my fellow classmates; finally, after giving me a hug and a kiss, she left with a gentle "Goodbye."

It was all standard nursery school procedure—everybody's mom did pretty much the same thing—but, apparently, the message hadn't gotten to Abe. (Or, just as likely, he'd chosen to ignore it.) Either way, none of that touchy-feely stuff happened on the morning in question. Instead, Abe pulled up to the curb near the school's entrance. Then, without moving from his position behind the wheel, he leaned across the front bench-seat where I was sitting and opened the passenger side door so I could make a quick exit.

It took me a moment to grasp the full import of Abe's plan, which involved my attempting a first-ever solo journey across the front lawn, through the open courtyard and from there to a classroom whose location I wasn't entirely confident of finding. It was far and away the most frightening idea I'd ever considered.

"What!" I remember thinking to myself. "You aren't coming with me? You want me to go in there all by myself? Does my mom know about this?"

Of course, I never actually verbalized any of these questions, and, frankly, I don't think it would have done much good. Abe certainly hadn't noticed how big my eyes had suddenly become or how much my lower lip was starting to quiver. Even if he had, he wouldn't have been likely to acknowledge those kinds of unmanly feelings anyway. Instead, as I sat frozen in the car, still peering nervously through the gaping open door, Abe leaned over, looked me in the eye, and simply said, "Bye."

"Holy Shit!" I nearly screamed. "I'm a dead man!"

Okay, so maybe my almost 4-year-old vocabulary had yet to include that particular expletive, but the expression does adequately capture my state of mind as I looked again through the open car door. Ahead of me lay the most perilous journey of my life, and the odds of surviving were thin. It was like being sent into the valley of the shadow of death but without the Shepherd. It was like walking on the moon but without a spacesuit. It was like … well, you get the idea.

I realize this introduction to Abe may sound a bit harsh. A more charming version would have featured me sitting on Abe's lap while he read stories to me in front of the fireplace. The problem, though, is that those memories don't exist, because Abe didn't do those sorts of things. Unlike my other three grandparents, Abe was never the giver of unconditional love—in his mind that was something Labrador retrievers did. With Abe, love, like everything else in life, had to be earned.

I don't want to overstate Abe's sternness or exaggerate his no-nonsense attitude. Compared to my dad, for example, Abe was a paragon of emotional availability, but compared to my other grandparents he was singularly different. No doubt when I was very young, Abe would have played better if his edges were softer. But that's not who he was.

Abe saw the world differently than just about anyone else. Where my other grandfather, Grampy, embraced nearly every opportunity for social gathering, Abe saw only uncomfortable conversations and dull subject matter. Where Bee looked out at their huge back yard in Grover Beach and envisioned an orchard with room for a garden, Abe saw (and I'm not making this up) a business opportunity to raise earthworms. And where Grammie might look appreciatively at the beauty of the forest, Abe would stomp through the trees and underbrush fully armed and ready to kill something for dinner.

He was a Manly Man from head to toe, and Abe prided himself on fulfilling that image. To be sure, it was a role more limiting than he ever realized, but where he was good he was very, very good. And to the great surprise of his sons and contemporaries, Abe would eventually become a very good grandfather. Partially, he just fit better with older children, but the bigger reason was that in the last two decades of his life Abe managed to grow as a person—and that would make all the difference.

Abe and the author in a make-do sandbox, 1955. Dressed in business attire and smoking a cigarette, Abe's first years as a grandfather were as awkward as this picture suggests.

CHAPTER 22

Bee's Hands

While I have a scattering of memories that go all the way back to my two-year-old self, it wasn't until I was nearly five that my grandmother Bee appears, and even then, it isn't her face that I see, it's her hands. This is unexpectedly more appropriate than one might guess, because—in exactly the kind of irony the Universe seems to enjoy—Bee's hands help explain how extraordinary she really was.

From a few steps away, they looked ordinary. Bee's hands were average size and average color, but up close they were different. Every knuckle looked like it had been made with a big irregular shaped marble, and if you looked carefully most of her fingers were crooked. Her skin, which was wrinkled, blotchy, and impossibly thin, added to the overall effect, but what impressed me the most was that Bee's hands shook all the time.

It wasn't violent shaking, and they would stop altogether the moment she held onto something solid or heavy, but if her hands were dangling by her side or trying to pick up something small and light they moved as if they were attached to some kind of slow-motion vibrator. It was a movement nobody else could make, and as a little boy I was in awe. As hard as I tried, I could never make my hands shake for more than a few seconds, and never with the same jiggle Bee had.

However, what really made Bee's hands magical happened in the kitchen. They were like a commercial appliance. When everyone else got out a mixer, for things like pancake batter, frosting, or pudding, Bee simply put all the ingredients in a bowl, placed a big fork in one of her shaking hands, directed it towards the bowl and let it go to work. Or so I thought.

Even more impressive (in my little-boy mind) was Bee's bologna sandwich-making prowess. Growing up I thought everybody on the planet had a bologna sandwich for lunch (I had one every day until I was ten years old, after that I had two), and nobody could make a bologna sandwich faster than my grandmother. With an awesome display of effortless efficiency, Bee would hold a slice of bread in one shaking hand, and in the other shaking hand, a butter knife. She'd dip the shaking knife into an open jar of mayonnaise, where it instantly coated itself, then, bring both shaking hands into close proximity and "poof" the bread was covered. Nobody else had a grandmother who could do that!

It would be years before I understood that it was arthritis (not marbles) that had swollen and deformed Bee's knuckles, that her fingers hurt all the time, and that every morning she clutched a big heavy mug of hot coffee in order to warm her stiff hands before massaging each joint and slowly coaxing it into movement. That palsy, which caused her hands to shake, denied her the ability to perform even the simplest task requiring fine motor skills—even with one hand holding the other to help steady it, she could barely scrawl an illegible signature.

But here's the thing. In the more than forty years I knew her, Bee never once complained about her hands. Not once. It was as though she'd been given a handicap she refused to accept. Instead, whenever they became a problem, she ignored them if possible and used workarounds for everything else.

With those hands Bee raised two sons and helped a string of family businesses succeed. As a grandmother they were the hands that got down on the floor to play blocks with her grandchildren. A generation later they were the hands that held her first great-grandchild, Amy, with a newfound joy in the miracle of life, and more than 20 years after that, near the end of Bee's long life they were the hands—full of every kindness her soul possessed—that reached up in gentle reassurance to touch the face of her great-granddaughter, Bethany.

CHAPTER 23

Abe and Bee's House

In the early 1960s Saturday night signaled the end of the workweek, and at least once a month both the Lee Miner and Glenn Miner households, eager for some adult time, would enthusiastically deposit my entire generation at Abe and Bee's house for the night. By 1961 there were five of us: myself age 9, followed by my sister, Kitty, 7; our cousins, Kim and Teri 7 and 6; and, finally, my little brother, Steve, 4.

We'd all arrive by late afternoon and immediately head for Bee's kitchen. Just past the front door off the main hallway, the kitchen was the largest room in the house. Partially divided by a short wall, one end contained the dining room set—a big brown Formica table with vinyl-cushioned chairs—and a view out the large front window. The other end contained cupboards, counters, Coppertone-colored appliances, and the cookie jar.

Ah! The cookie jar. That magical vessel sitting high atop the counter next to the stove—always full of the most freshly baked and delicious chocolate chip cookies the world has ever known. Even its color spoke of enchantment.

All right, "enchantment" might be a stretch—it was more of a 1950s never-to-be-repeated shade of pink, which didn't exactly complement Coppertone (or any other color for that matter)—so perhaps "inexplicable" would be more accurate, but, really, none of that mattered. Standing on tiptoes, I was just tall enough to reach up and pull it to the edge of the counter. I still couldn't see anything inside, but I quickly became an expert at exploring every cookie with my fingertips and finding a big one.

All by itself the cookie jar would have made our stay at Abe and Bee's house worthwhile, but it was just the prelude (albeit a really, really good prelude) to the major event of the evening, dinner.

As a group, my generation of Miners was notoriously picky about food. Indeed, with the notable exception of myself (who was eternally hungry and eager to eat anything that wasn't a lima bean), the rest of my siblings and cousins had more self-imposed dietary restrictions than anyone I had ever met.[26]

As I recall, the only dinner item we could all agree on was spaghetti, and even that failed because our respective moms made the sauce differently. Looking back from the perspective of an ordinary parent, I'm not sure how I would have solved this dinner dilemma, but it would likely have involved peanut butter and jelly sandwiches, Top Ramen, and a stern helping of ultimatum.

But that's not what happened at Abe and Bee's. In a brilliant display of problem solving, Bee hit upon a solution that would

---

26 Of course, I had yet to meet my future daughters, but that's another story ...

only have occurred to a grandmother: she fixed a separate meal for everyone.

So, shortly after our arrival and a quick afternoon snack of milk and the aforementioned best chocolate chip cookies in the world, we all piled into Abe and Bee's Carryall and headed to the market.

Aptly named Young's Giant Food it was the newest and biggest building in town—the first supermarket our community had ever

A MINER SIDE NOTE

THE CARRYALL

A forerunner to today's sport-utility vehicles, Abe and Bee's circa 1960 Chevy Suburban Carryall put a heavy emphasis on utility—meaning it was missing nearly every amenity found on today's automobiles. Forget conveniences like cruise control and cup holders (they had yet to be invented); this vehicle was so utilitarian it didn't even have passenger doors or passenger seats.

Seriously, other than the single bench seat in the front, where Abe and Bee sat, the rest of the vehicle was an empty metal box with side windows and large panel doors in the rear.

Thoughtfully, Abe always kept a couple of old sleeping bags laid across the corrugated metal floor of the cargo area, which provided "Festival Seating" for all the grandkids.

seen. About half the size of today's supermarkets, it was still huge for its day, and just going there was a treat. It contained so much stuff, so many aisles, and such tall displays, that it was easy to get lost—and, as five excited little grandchildren, we sometimes did. But the real treat was that, as long as we didn't choose candy, each of us could pick out anything we wanted for dinner.

Once everyone had made their dinner selections, it was back to Abe and Bee's house, where Abe would attempt to monitor all the grandkids playing in the living room, while Bee got out an assortment of cast iron skillets and began frying five different meals along with whatever she and Abe were having for dinner.

Sometimes we'd eat in the living room with our plates atop foldable TV trays as we watched the latest sitcom. Usually, however, we were all gathered around the kitchen table eating and talking. But, whatever the circumstance, as soon as dinner was over and the plates were cleared, it was time for dessert.

While not as picky about dessert, neither was this group capable of arriving at consensus between the standard choices. So, in a second ingenious solution (this one by Abe), dessert was almost always Neapolitan ice cream, and whoever didn't like one of the flavors in their bowl could always make a deal with a sibling or cousin for a different flavor.

"I'll trade you all my chocolate for half your strawberry. No, wait, make that half my chocolate for all of your vanilla, or maybe ..." and so it went.

But, as good as Saturday evening was—cookies, dinner, ice cream, and playing in a living room full of kids—Sunday morning was usually better.

Immediately after breakfast (remarkably, everyone agreed on bacon, eggs, and pancakes), we were off on an adventure. Often this was a trip to the sand dunes, which in my mind is still one of nature's best amusement parks. There we could play hide and seek for days or roll down the steeper dunes and get so much sand in our shoes we'd have to stop and empty them out before we could walk again. Safaris were also popular—wandering through the tall grass, climbing the towering peaks, and peering into the forbidden swamp.

Other times, we'd stop to feed the ducks at the Oceano Lagoon, which, when we were all very young, was a particularly exciting near-death experience.

Standing by the shore with two or three loaves of bread between us, we'd begin breaking the bread into small pieces and throwing them on the ground. Almost immediately the first ducks would arrive, followed shortly by more ducks, then more ducks again, and soon they'd all be advancing towards us en masse (our estimates ran into the thousands). Unable to keep up with the demand, we'd begin a tactical retreat. With each backward step the bread-dispensing became more hurried and the pieces of bread ever larger. Soon we were throwing entire slices until, finally, abandoning all hope and whatever bread was left, we'd run back to the safety of the Carryall.

There were other adventures as well, but the one that was probably the best was also the simplest—walking along the shoreline. There were sand dollars and seashells to collect, clams and sand crabs to dig up, and flocks of shorebirds to chase. Best of all, there were waves, and the lure of the ocean constantly rushing towards us and then just as quickly rushing away would eventually prove irresistible. Soon we'd be playing tag with the ocean—a game ultimately lost by every kid who's ever participated, but, then, isn't that the best part?

At Abe and Bee's there was always adventure, the cookie jar was always full, and everything came with an extra helping of love.

CHAPTER 24

Grammie and Grampy

I t's hard to overstate how different each of our grandparents was. Of course, *everyone* was different from Abe, but as children that had yet to become apparent. Looking at our respective grandfathers, they seemed similar enough: they were both about the same size and shape; they both worked; they both went fishing whenever possible. Our grandmothers, however, were easy to tell apart.

Bee looked every bit the Scandinavian: tall, blue-eyed, and blond. Grammie, though still having a pleasant appearance, was short, stout, and dark; but as different as they looked on the outside, it was nothing compared to their personalities. Although, when you consider the three lead female characters in our family at this time—Mom, Bee and Grammie—perhaps being completely different was some kind of precondition for membership.

Look again at the *Good Housekeeping* version of femininity on page 134 and consider: Mom, though partially ensnared by the expectations it represented, railed against its absurdity; Bee deliberately and completely ignored every part of it, while Grammie found the entire concept aspirational.

In Grammie's world women were supposed to look and act just as the magazine add suggested. So, whether Grammie was doing the laundry, attending a formal dinner, or baking something in the oven, she wore shoes with heels and a dress with a petticoat all day, every day.

It was actually worse than that, because, along with her dress code, Grammie also adhered to a very long list of things ladies didn't do. They didn't go fishing; they didn't care much for adventure; and, they *never ever* got dirty. There were other rules as well, but those last two alone had a rather limiting effect on our relationship. I mean, really, to a little boy, if it wasn't an adventure and you couldn't get dirty, well, what was the point?

There was, however, one spectacular benefit to Grammie's *Good Housekeeping* view of the world, which was obvious every time we visited. Her kitchen was Pastry Heaven.

Honestly, it may well have *been* Pastry Heaven, because in all the years since nothing has ever measured up to those remembered tastes and smells. There was always some kind of pie, often a cake, and, for any excuse at all, homemade chocolate éclairs. And that was just the everyday stuff! For special occasions—and Grammie could make anything a special occasion—there was Boston Cream pie, cupcakes, triple-layer cake, and graham cracker sandwiches (imagine a big square Oreo cookie with homemade frosting in the middle).

All of it was delicious, and I remain truly and deeply appreciative for every cookie, cupcake, and piece of pie I ever received from her kitchen. It seems, however, that all that cooking must have been exceedingly time-consuming, because Grammie in the kitchen—with a frilly apron over a frilly dress—fills up almost all my childhood memories of her. For Grampy I have memories without end…

*   *   *   *

From the perspective of a young boy, everything about Grampy's job was wonderfully exciting, and from age 6 to somewhere in my early teens, I would accompany him to work once or twice a year. He'd wake me up just after 2 in the morning, and, while I stumbled around in the dark trying to wake up and get dressed, Grampy would make us both a cup of hot chocolate and some toast for the ride down to the Spot (the warehouse he shared with another dealer).

We'd typically arrive as the delivery truck was unloading, and watch uncountable bundles of newspapers fly out the back of the truck, where waiting carriers stacked them according to section—Sports, Metro, Classified, etc. These would then be stuffed by hand, one into the other along with advertising inserts, then folded in half, and the finished product tied with string by the most incredible machine I'd ever seen.

Called the Knotter, it was a mechanical contraption of gears, pulleys, whirling motors, and a large spool of string attached to a mechanical arm. Inserting a folded newspaper into the Knotter would trigger the arm, which instantly came down, wrapped a piece of string around the paper, and tied it in a knot so tight it couldn't be untied.

By itself the un-tieable knot was completely amazing, but by far the most memorable attribute of the Knotter was how dangerous it was. I remember listening with a mix of anxiety and fascination as Grampy explained its safety features—there weren't any. There were no safety guards, cutoff switches, or pressure sensors. Nothing. You either operated the Knotter exactly as demonstrated or it jammed …

if you were lucky. If you were unlucky, it tied the string *through* your hand.

To this day the Knotter's awe-inspiring interplay of complexity and lethality remains unmatched. Fortunately, for me and all those carriers, its operation was pretty straight-forward, and, though I did produce more than my share of mangled papers and jammed machinery, all my digits survived.

By 4 a.m. the Spot was usually empty, and each carrier, with a car full of about 400 papers (which they had assembled, folded, and tied with the Knotter) was speeding towards their assigned neighborhoods. Really good carriers would open both the driver and passenger side windows, drive zigzag down the street and throw papers out both windows. The best carrier ever was a man named Don, who always threw two routes and worked nearly 20 years as a carrier because he kept getting fired from his day job. He alone owned an old convertible, and with the top down he would steer the car with his knees, drive straight down the middle of the street, and, using both arms, throw papers to the driveways on either side.

As Grampy's occasional helper, I dreaded the delivery portion of the job; it always made me carsick. Sitting in the back seat, squished between mountains of newspapers, my job was to continuously move the papers to the front seat, where Grampy could reach them easily to throw out the open windows. With the car lurching from side to side, all I could see was newspapers and the back of the front seat. At the end of each block we'd round the corner at high speed (pushing me and all the papers to one side), then lurch down the next street.

I particularly remember one morning when, for the first and only time, Kitty (who was about 8 years old at this time) accompanied us. Apparently, Grampy had expected to throw one route that morning, but a second carrier called in sick and he ended up with two. That meant the car had to be loaded with more papers than I'd ever seen stuffed into a vehicle. Other than a small space for Grampy behind the steering wheel, the rest of the car was nothing but newspapers. Even the trunk was full of newspapers. There was nowhere for Kitty and me to sit, so we climbed over and through a sea of papers towards the back window and managed to squeeze into the tiny space between the top of the newspapers and the headliner of the car. Off we went.

It was wonderfully exciting driving towards the first route. Kitty and I could see Grampy and, through his rolled-down window, a little bit of the street, but the rest of our world consisted only of newspapers and whatever material the headliner was made from. Soon we arrived at the route's beginning point, Grampy threw out the first paper and all the lurching and turning began. Kitty, who was even more prone to motion sickness than I was, lasted about five blocks before informing Grampy she was going to throw up. He stopped in a panic and solved the problem by depositing both us at the next corner.

"I'll be back in 20 minutes," Grampy shouted as he drove back into the night. "Don't move from this corner!"

Standing under the streetlamp, we were both supremely relieved to be out of the car, but almost immediately realized we were completely lost and utterly alone in the middle of LA, in the middle of the night, and we were starting to freeze to death.

After what felt like hours, Grampy returned and we eagerly jumped into the warmth and safety of the back seat, or at least that general area. It was still covered with hundreds of newspapers, we still could barely see outside, and immediately the lurching and turning resumed just as before.

Ten minutes later we were back on another street corner. And so it went: car, street corner; car, street corner; until finally the papers were gone and it was time to go home. Kitty never went with us again.

By 6 a.m., barring a calamity, all the papers were delivered. The carriers had all gone home (or to their next job), and it was time for breakfast, which, if his grandchildren were present, meant donuts.

Having already survived two heart attacks, Grampy wasn't supposed to eat donuts, but as long as we didn't tell Grammie, he was willing to make an exception.

Actually, when it came to donuts, exceptions seemed to be the rule, because no matter which donut shop we visited, he always knew the employees and customers. (I'm afraid Grampy was similarly dismissive about his pack-a-day cigarette habit and being 50-plus pounds overweight. True, the benefits of a healthy lifestyle weren't fully understood in the mid-20th century, but I doubt that would have mattered. Grampy knew what he liked and it's unlikely science would have changed his mind.)

By 7 a.m. Grampy was back home—ready for the second half of his day. In an office next to the garage he answered the phone, did paperwork, and, later in the morning, hand-delivered the "misses"— papers the carriers had mistakenly thrown in the bushes, the sprinklers, to the wrong address, etc. Then, after a big lunch, he'd take a nap from about one to three o'clock in the afternoon. When he arose, the rest of each day was free to spend with family and friends until his typical bedtime around 10 p.m.

*　　*　　*　　*

As mentioned earlier, Grammie and Grampy lived in Culver City, which was about a four-hour drive from the Central Coast. Typically, our family traveled to their house over Christmas vacation and the three of us kids spent a week or more there each summer. Other holidays varied, but the upshot of this long-distance schedule was that whenever we saw Grammie and Grampy it was usually a special occasion, and Grampy was always determined to make sure something special happened.[27]

There were fishing trips, Dodgers games, and our very own tree house. There was a restaurant that served apple pie for lunch, and the adventure of the newspaper business, but the Grand Prize of all my memories with Grampy was and will always remain Disneyland.

It was an annual ritual, and each summer Grampy would take Kitty, Steve, and me to that Magic Kingdom.[28] It was the highlight of every one of my formative years, and even today I find myself completely and irrationally excited about the place. There wasn't a ride I didn't like or a character I didn't love. I remember the Mule Ride, the Rocket Ship to the Moon, and the House of the Future—attractions long since

---

27　Grammie and Grampy believed birthdays were especially important, and throughout our childhood, Kitty, Steve and I could always count on them both being there on those special days (along with multiple presents).

28　Occasionally, Grammie accompanied us, but usually it was just Grampy.

retired. I remember E-tickets, my first ride on the Matterhorn, driving my first car in Autopia, the shooting gallery—the list goes on and on—but as outstanding as they all were, my best memory of Disneyland remains Tom Sawyer's Island.

After spending the morning running from ride to ride, we'd all board Tom Sawyer's raft and arrive on the island just after lunch. It was here that Grampy, conditioned by decades of nap-taking and knowing he had to survive until the fireworks display at 9 p.m., would station himself on a shady bench right next to the island's only exit and, after giving Kitty, Steve, and me a very stern warning not to leave the island under any conditions, would promptly fall asleep.

For the next 90 minutes or so, the three of us were on our own. There were mountains to climb, secret forest trails to wander through, and a trading post to investigate. There were caves to explore and get lost in, forts to defend, Indians to shoot, and a rickety suspension bridge to cross if you dared. It was an island of legends where Huckleberry Finn, Davy Crockett, Captain Hook, Wendy, and Pocahontas were all just around the corner!

I realize there are those who do not share my enthusiasm for Disneyland and are likely to dismiss all its joys as a brazen, corporate-driven manipulation of human emotions. What a shame those poor skeptics never experienced Disneyland with Grampy as their guide.

Regardless, I remain convinced that a timeless enchantment infuses the entire park, and never was that special magic more in evidence than some 50 years after my first visit, when on a warm summer morning I found myself once again aboard the raft to Tom Sawyer's Island.

Standing next to me, atop a pile of stacked wooden boxes, was my nearly 3-year-old grandson, Giacomo, and, as we chugged across the river towards our destination, he leaned into me for balance and reassurance.

It was an extraordinary moment and in my own excitement I tried to convey to Giacomo why our destination was so special.

"When I was a little boy," I began, "my grandfather used to take me to Tom Sawyer's Island." I paused for a moment before adding, "and when your daddy was a little boy, he went to Tom Sawyer's Island."

A MINER SIDE NOTE

EXTRAORDINARY MOMENTS

In my experience, the Universe presents each of us with a few *Extraordinary Moments*. They can be triggered by something as important as holding your firstborn child, or as mundane as a solitary walk. But whatever the reason, at the instant of their happening, time comes to a standstill. Past and future blend together, and every part of your being—every memory, every experience, every hope—suddenly becomes the present.

Extraordinary Moments are over almost as soon as they begin; but, that "Aha!" instant can last a lifetime. They're the emotional equivalent of being slapped by someone who means it, and somewhere deep inside you can hear the Universe shouting,

"PAY ATTENTION!"

Giacomo looked at the island, then looked again at me. Being a particularly bright little boy, he realized there was some kind of a pattern to my statements, and even if he wasn't quite sure how they connected, he certainly sensed my excitement. He thought a moment longer and then, in a voice full of satisfaction and a grin suggesting he had just solved one of life's most interesting puzzles, Giacomo replied, "And I a little boy too!"

It was all I could have hoped for, and, just as we reached the shore of Tom Sawyer's Island to disembark, I picked him up, gave him the biggest hug his excitement would allow, and we were off.

Somewhere in the distance I could feel Grampy smiling.

*   *   *   *

In Grampy's world *Life Was Good*, and in the company of other adults his conviction was often contagious. For his grandchildren, the effect was even stronger. Probably owing to his own distressing childhood, Grampy was always eager to become engaged in ours. More than that, he had a childlike ability to see freshness in the world—to be "oohed" and "aahed" by surprise and adventure, and to the everlasting delight of his grandsons, one of Grampy's favorite adventures was taking us fishing.[29]

Most of those fishing adventures were on a chartered boat out of San Pedro Harbor, where, on warm summer nights, we'd drift far

---

29 In everything else, Grampy always included Kitty. But, like nearly everyone in his generation, he believed that girls didn't go fishing. On those manly adventures, Kitty always stayed home. There, under Grammie's tutelage, she became an accomplished cook and seamstress—skills she still possesses. Sadly, (through no fault of Grampy's), neither of her brothers ever became very good at fishing.

offshore, barely able to see the twinkling lights of LA, but, as with most experiences, the first one remains the best, and my very first memory of fishing with Grampy happened the day after my 6th birthday.

We left early in the morning to follow a mountain road that even today seems to exhibit a powerful aversion to straightaways. This was our first great adventure together and, after driving for what seemed to me like days without end, we finally arrived at Lake Cachuma (ka-chew-ma), perched high above the coastal city of Santa Barbara.

A few days earlier Grampy had left his boat at the marina, and we quickly parked the car, grabbed our gear, and climbed aboard. To my 6-year-old sensibilities, Grampy's 17-foot aluminum fishing boat was enormous. It also had an enormous silver outboard motor with *Johnson* boldly printed on the cowling. Of course, I couldn't yet read *Johnson,* but I remember being rather disappointed upon learning that all those letters didn't spell *Grampy.*

I couldn't understand why he put someone else's name on *his* motor, and things got even more confusing when I noticed another group of even bigger letters on the back of the boat.

"That's the boat's name," my grandfather explained. "It spells *Peggie T,* which stands for your grandmother's maiden name."

None of this made any sense to me, but I do remember being rather uneasy about my grandmother's "maiden-ness." Was it something I might catch? Had my parents simply been too embarrassed to tell me about it? What did it mean?

It was all so typical of adult behavior and further proof that grownups were just trying to be difficult. After all, if you wanted a boat named for my grandmother, then call it *Grammie,* and if you went to the trouble of putting all those letters on a big silver motor, then make it spell *Grampy*. Why go out of your way to confuse everything? I was still trying to resolve all these problems when, suddenly, the big, misnamed *Johnson* motor sprang to life. Grampy looked over at me with a twinkle in his eye and asked, "Hey, Mikey can you help me drive this boat?"

"Can you help me drive this boat?" Are you kidding me?! I mean really, in all of creation could there be a more glorious question for a little boy? Even now, looking back from more than 60 years, I still smile every time I remember Grampy's question, and I can tell you honestly that, if today I was somehow presented with a choice between piloting the *Starship Enterprise* or driving the *Peggie T* for the first time again, I'd be back sitting on Grampy's lap and reliving that perfect afternoon.

I probably baited my first hook and caught my first fish on that trip, but all I really remember was driving the *Peggie T*. True, I was a bit disappointed with the throttle, which was located next to the steering wheel. The further you pushed the lever, the faster the boat went, but it was made wrong. No matter how hard I pushed, the lever only moved a short distance before it stopped, and the boat wouldn't go any faster. Clearly, we needed a bigger lever. Yet, despite this manufacturing defect and the awkward fact that, even sitting on Grampy's lap, I could barely see where we were going, it was still marvelous!

We went down the lake, up the lake, across the lake, and every direction in between. Behind us, like some new kind of white shadow that had attached itself to the boat, a huge wake of water followed. Even now, if I close my eyes for just a second, I can see the foamy white of our wake and feel the vibration of the boat and the sideways force of every "S" turn we made. It may have been the best day of my entire life, and when we arrived back at the dock late that afternoon I was blissfully exhausted. Unfortunately, this is where my memory of the day ends, which is a shame, because the ending is the best part. But for that we will need to rely on my grandfather's frequent retelling of what happened next.

According to Grampy, by the time we docked the boat and put everything back in the car, I could barely keep my eyes open. We both climbed into the front seat and readied ourselves for the long drive home, which, because this was 1958 and no one had yet conceived of things like personal safety or product liability, meant that Grampy simply checked to make sure my door was closed, then lit up his first cigarette, while I sat next to him and stared at the solid metal dashboard in front of me.

It would never have occurred to me (or anyone else in that decade) what a monumental task my immune system was about to perform in protecting my lungs from airborne carcinogens, or how much at risk I'd be without a seat belt, padded dashboard or air bags. However, it did occur to me that the long front bench seat of the car would make a much better bed than a chair. So I laid down, put my head on Grampy's lap, and, just before falling fast asleep, looked up at him in complete innocence and said, "I'm sure gonna miss you when you die."

Apparently, that comment made a lasting impression on my grandfather, because for the rest of his life Grampy never tired of retelling this story. He'd go into all the details, saving my final remark until the end, then finish with his own heartfelt observation.

"It was the nicest thing anybody ever said to me!"

CHAPTER 25

The Perils of Parenting

When it comes to dealing with children, especially young children, grandparents have a decided advantage over mere mothers and fathers. I know. I've served tours of duty in both positions, and believe me, it's good to be a grandparent.

Of course, all by itself, the 24-hour return policy most grandparents enjoy is hard to overstate. Yet, as lovely as that option might be, the real advantage to grandparenting isn't a lack of responsibility.

It's an abundance of experience.

As a grandparent I know diapers will end, school will start, and that neither scraped knees nor splinters are fatal. I know it's silly to sweat the small stuff and that most of what looks like big stuff isn't.

Mere parents, on the other hand, are not so lucky. When I first became a new father, I was clueless, frightened, and, by the end of that first sleepless week, convinced my doom would be eternal. It nearly was, because, in one of life's dumbest ironies, I spent most of next 20 years being one step behind the parental learning curve … and then our children left home.

By any measure, parenting is a tough job. In fact, it may be the toughest job there is, and just surviving counts for some measure of success. Still, like most every other life skill, parental ability varies widely. A few take to it naturally; for some of us it can be a constant challenge. And, as we're about to see, there are those who seem never to get the hang of it at all …

*   *   *   *

Just after Kitty turned 3 years old, in what would prove to be her earliest and most vivid memory, Mom rushed her to the hospital emergency room with multiple head wounds.

Fortunately, by the time they arrived at the ER, Kitty had mostly stopped crying, her head had mostly stopped bleeding, and, once the doctor had determined there was nothing life-threatening in her injuries, Mom had mostly calmed down and was beginning to regain her composure.

Unfortunately, Mom's slowly returning sense of well-being, which was already in a delicate balance, quickly unraveled when, to the doctor's question as to how the injury was sustained, Kitty exclaimed, "Mikey hit me on the head with the garden rake!"

Apparently, the doctor, who thought he'd heard everything, was somewhat shocked by this explanation, but his reaction was nothing compared to Mom's.

She was apoplectic. Caught between mortification and bewilderment, Mom struggled to make sense of Kitty's accusation against her 4-and-1/2-year-old brother, but nothing worked. Finally, she managed a feeble, "But Kitty, surely it must have been an accident."

"No!" Kitty replied with conviction. "He did it on purpose!"

Poor Mom. She couldn't begin to resolve the facts she was being clobbered with. Up until this moment she'd always assumed her children were more or less normal. Certainly, she'd observed the occasional fight between Kitty and myself, but, so far as Mom was aware, neither of us had ever before used lethal force against one another. What the hell was going on?!

Not surprisingly, this very question was uppermost on Mom's mind, and when she and Kitty finally returned home from the hospital, Mom immediately got eyeball to eyeball with me to begin her interrogation.

Given the circumstances—a little sister with bits of dried blood still clinging to her curly blond hair, who is literally pointing the "finger of guilt" in your direction, along with a mother who is obviously wondering if reform school might be her best option—I think it safe to assume that most 4-and-1/2-year-olds would have been terrified.

Not me. I had the confidence of the completely innocent. There was no way I could be in trouble. And, to Mom's question as to just how Kitty's head had come into contact with the garden rake, I readily admitted my role as the perpetrator along with a simple explanation: "Daddy told me I could!"

It was right about here, I believe, that Mom's higher-level brain functions completely went offline. Nothing was making any sense, because in her carefully ordered universe none of this could have happened.

Sadly, it would turn out that Mom's fundamental mistake lay not in logic but in assumptions, specifically her belief that Dad was living in the same universe as she was (or at least one nearby) and that he shared the same parental sensibilities. Neither would prove to be true.

We'll get to Dad's universe in a moment, but, regarding his parental sensibilities, I'm afraid all evidence suggests he simply didn't have any. Indeed, only the week before, he had unwittingly dispensed some of the worst parental advice ever recorded when, on one of the rare occasions Dad was actually home and available, I had approached him with the biggest problem of my young life. The boy down the street was bullying me and I didn't know how to make him stop.

Even now I can remember Dad carefully pondering this question. While his response was without doubt honest and sincere, it wasn't exactly tailored to his audience. Instead, he considered the problem from his own perspective, which, in 1956 at age 29, was that of a soldier turned family breadwinner. In his view, the world was a serious place where no man could let himself be pushed around.

"When someone's bothering you," he began, "you tell them to stop. If they don't, you tell them to stop a second time. The third time you hit them."

This sounded like the wisest thing I'd ever heard. It was short, direct, and something I could remember. Besides, it must be true because it came from Dad, who was the biggest, strongest, and smartest man alive.

Still, I was a bit apprehensive when it came to actually applying Dad's advice, because I wasn't entirely convinced he understood how huge the boy down the street really was. It therefore seemed prudent to test this new directive in an environment that would afford some measure of personal safety.

Two days later, Kitty presented herself.

For reasons I no longer remember (but were surely virtuous), I had decided to plant a garden in our un-landscaped backyard.[30] To that end I had gathered together the shovel, hoe, and rake—every tool our small garage contained—and was busily engaged in clearing the land when Kitty arrived eager to participate. Naturally, I didn't want my little sister involved in my new project and, with rake in hand, I told her to leave.

Just as naturally, Kitty wasn't about to take orders from me and immediately picked up the shovel and began "helping" me. Still holding the rake, I told her to leave a second time. No response. So, after double-checking my math, I let go with the rake, making sure the pointy ends were facing down.

For the record, I want to acknowledge that I'm not particularly proud of this childhood episode (although it was impressively effective). Moreover, Mom's continuous and booming lecture of "Never hit your sister!" delivered in wrath-of-god mode for what seemed like days on end did leave a lasting impression. Kitty and I never came to blows again—or at least nothing that involved weapons.

Dad, I believe, fared less well. I'm not sure what conversations passed between him and Mom, but they couldn't have been enjoyable. It was (and I mean this quite literally) the last time he ever gave me any advice.

Poor Dad. Few men (and I'm pretty sure no women at all) have ever become parents with fewer innate skills. He was, and for the most part

---

30 Our family had only recently moved to Grover Beach, and we were living in a small rental house near the railroad tracks.

would remain, clueless. Unhappily, his social skills in general weren't much better. Perhaps he'd spent too much time alone in the desert, or maybe he'd inherited too much of his father's solitary personality, but whatever the cause, Dad was almost always out of sync with his environment.

In familiar circumstances and with familiar people, he could function almost normally, but put him in a room full of strangers with no script to follow and Dad simply had no idea what to say or do. None. Additionally, Dad also seemed to suffer from what might best be described as temporal dislocation—he always thought he should be living in a world that included Andy Burnett.

If that last sentence isn't particularly enlightening, you're in good company. Almost no one alive today has ever heard of Mr. Burnett, because he existed only as a fictional character in a book long out of print.

The main character in *The Saga of Andy Burnett*—a historical novel, based loosely on facts, and set in the wilderness west of the Mississippi River sometime around 1820—Andy Burnett lived in a world with no roads, no towns and no people other than the occasional adversary, usually played by a Native American. A precursor to the cowboy archetype, Andy was young, solitary, and self-reliant. He followed a strict moral code, survived through cunning and perseverance, and lived a life of continuous adventure and discovery.

It was Dad's favorite book. He reread it every few years, and each time found himself longing to be the hero, which wasn't as much of a stretch as it might sound. At 6 foot, 2 inches, Dad was tall, athletic, and ruggedly handsome. Added to those physical characteristics were his remarkable skills in hunting and fishing, along with a near obsession for the outdoors. The result being that, to his overall appearance and demeanor, if one could have added a deerskin jacket and a coonskin hat, Dad would have easily passed for Daniel Boone.

Truthfully, he might have surpassed Daniel Boone and would certainly have bested Andy Burnett because, along with his Mountain Man physique and skills, Dad was absolutely extraordinary with animals. Dogs, cats, horses: he could walk up to nearly any animal and in seconds gain its complete trust. Once (and I have witnesses) in just a few minutes Dad taught a small fish to swim onto his submerged hand, where it would lie still until he picked it up and dropped the fish back into the aquarium from a height of about 12 inches. It splashed happily to the bottom of the tank, then swam back up to do it again. Seriously, when it came to the outdoors in general and animals in particular, Dad was in a league of his own.

The problem, of course, was that Dad's unique and impressive talents, while undoubtedly lifesaving and even heroic if he ever found himself on the Lewis and Clark Expedition, were not particularly useful or valued in the late twentieth century.

In his own words, and a lament he voiced more than once, Dad was born a couple of hundred years too late—a mistake of Fate that would forever disappoint him.

But as short as he was on parenting skills, and as out of step as he often was in society, he seemed to find comfort in the role of family breadwinner, and in that capacity, until his late 30s, few people have ever worked harder at success.

CHAPTER 26

Growing Up with Mom

Of all my immediate ancestors, Mom was easily the smartest and best educated of the lot. She was also the most confusing. No doubt much of the fault was mine—lots of people confuse me—but Mom was special.

Sadly, all evidence suggests that she was just as befuddled with me as the other way around, and my long-held suspicion remains that much of our mutual confusion was simply a matter of gender.

You see, Mom was female, and by this, I mean she was *really* female. No doubt her own childhood played a leading role (i.e., 14 years of nothing but nuns for teachers and only girls for classmates would have left anyone with an unbalanced worldview). Mom, therefore, entered motherhood with no appreciation whatsoever for the rich and subtle workings of little-boy minds, which left her at something of a disadvantage when her firstborn child turned out to be male.

Given a perfect world and enough time, I'd like to think Mom would have eventually figured out the whole boy-girl thing, but neither of those conditions ever existed for her. First, from early motherhood until her children left home, she was either working full-time, going to college, doing post-graduate work or, some combination of the three.

At the best of times hers would have been a challenging schedule, and therein lies the second problem. Mom didn't live in the best of times. The traditional values she grew up with (and much of society reinforced) were forever in conflict with the life she found fulfilling.

Nevertheless, she remained a force to be reckoned with and to this day, whenever I search for the source of my own moral framework, I usually find Mom in the underpinnings.

*   *   *   *

Just before the start of second grade, when I was still 6 years old, our family moved from Grover Beach to Arroyo Grande—the town Mom and Dad would call home for the rest of their lives. To its citizens, and the few people outside the area who are even aware of its existence, Arroyo Grande is famous for just two things: 1) a few blocks of the old downtown, where a mix of buildings dating from the late 1800s have been tastefully intermingled with a few modern additions; and 2) a swinging footbridge that spans the creek connecting the old downtown with an adjacent neighborhood.

I know it's not much of a list, and when you add in the fact that, alone among the handful of cities that make up the Central Coast of California, only Arroyo Grande is missing a coastline, it's little wonder that my hometown never became the "Malibu of the North." Well, that and the fact some knucklehead named the place Arroyo Grande in the first place, which is Spanish for Big Ditch—a moniker that doesn't exactly lend itself to tourism.

Nevertheless, the local populace, myself included, remains inordinately proud of Arroyo Grande. There's a wholesomeness about the place that shows up in its tree-lined streets, the prolific display of flowers planted throughout the town by scores of volunteers, and the town's unofficial motto, "Arroyo Grande—Nice Place, Normal People."

It was here that I would grow up, meet my wife, and raise my own family, but all that was in some distant unknowable future. In the second grade my world consisted entirely of my immediate family and whatever was within a few block radius of home, because that's as far as Mom would let me venture out alone.

Back then all boys (and by this, I mean the five or six boys who lived nearby) roamed throughout the neighborhood whenever possible, and while none of us were as wholesome as the town we lived in, neither did any of us get arrested, killed, or even permanently maimed.

Arroyo Grande was sparsely populated at that time with far more vacant lots than there were houses. It wasn't quite like living in the country, but the abundance of wide-open spaces did allow some scope in our childhood adventures. We built forts everywhere, set fires occasionally, spied on girls, and caught every lizard, snake, and horny toad we could find. We could see a double feature movie for 25 cents on Saturday, go to the high school pool during the summer for another 25 cents. There was even an area next to the creek where bamboo grew in abundance, which, when lashed together properly and covered with an old blanket, made a superb Indian tepee and a perfect place for us all to become Blood Brothers.[31]

It was like living between the pages of *The Adventures of Huckleberry Finn,* and I would have instantly recognized myself if only I'd been big enough to read Mark Twain's book. Unhappily, it turned out that Mom had read that book, and she would prove to be far more adept in her parental role than Huck's Aunt Sally— particularly the part about me growing up "sivilized." To her credit, Mom would eventually enjoy some measure of success, but it wasn't easy... for either of us.

Likely, I played as big a role in these difficulties as did Mom's aforementioned lack of experience with boys, but the other contributing factor was the problem of "Grammie-ness," because Mom (just like Grammie) believed in a world where manners and decorum were observed by all, and everyone knew that "cleanliness was next to godliness."

Those ideals came with an ungodly long list of rules that, throughout my childhood, rarely made sense. Why, for instance, did I have to wear clean underwear every day, while my jacket hardly ever got washed— wasn't my jacket closer to dirt than my underwear? Or why did hands get washed before dinner, but faces washed after dinner—weren't they both touching my food?

---

31 Following an old and secret Indian ritual (handed down by older boys who knew about these sorts of things), two boys would each cut their own finger just enough to make it bleed. The participants would then press their respective bleeding fingers together, thereby mingling their blood and becoming Blood Brothers.

Basically (as far as I could tell) the problem centered on dirt: Mom believed there was something wrong if not outright evil about dirt, while I had a completely different understanding about the stuff. It was kind of a Zen thing. A wisdom if you will, shared by nearly all children, who at a very early age are able to grasp one of Nature's fundamental truths: *Everything Will Get Dirty*. For boys especially, dirt just *is*, and worrying about it only leads to suffering.

Sadly, Mom was never able to appreciate that simple fact, and whenever she saw me return home after a hard day at school or an afternoon spent roaming the neighborhood, her unfailingly shocked greeting was always,:

"HOW DID YOU GET SO DIRTY?"

It was a perpetual mystery. Most of the time I didn't even know I *was* dirty, and on the rare occasions when I was able to actually locate the offending grass stain on my pants or the mud on my shirt, I never once knew how they got there. To Mom's constant wonder, therefore, my answer was always an honest, "I don't know."

It was a strange ritual, yet no matter how many times we performed it, Mom was forever disappointed in its outcome. Except once. Or so it appeared, because for one glorious moment I thought we'd had a breakthrough.

I must have been 7 or 8 years old at the time when, in an insightful display of logic (which still seems remarkable for one so young), I arrived at a solution to Mom's problem with dirt. No longer would *getting* my clothes dirty be a problem. I'd simply wear my already dirty clothes over and over.

Eager to put my new plan into effect, I headed out the next morning for school, when Mom stopped me at the front door with instructions to return to my room and change into some clean clothes.

"But Mom," I pleaded, "They're just going to get dirty again."

In the face of this brilliant and self-evident truth, Mom was momentarily dumbfounded. She just stood there looking at me with a mixture of disappointment and disbelief before finally replying, "That's like saying, 'Why take a bath?' You're just going to get dirty again."

"Exactly!" I responded with enthusiasm, and for just that instant I thought Mom had experienced an epiphany. Finally, all the wasted time spent bathing and hand washing and changing clothes was at an end.

I was wrong. Instead of Mom nodding her head in agreement as expected, a look not unlike horror spread across her face, an unintelligible sound escaped from her lips, and in a gesture of near total despair, she threw up her arms—presumably in the hope of divine intervention.

Alas, the gods of understanding never arrived, and, though I would continue my attempts for many years to come, all efforts to educate Mom about clothes and baths and dirt were doomed. She never got any of it.

Which is not to suggest she gave up—Mom never wavered in her cleanliness/godliness rules. Neither did she overlook any of my numerous other character defects, and throughout my childhood Mom worked tirelessly to reform them. [32]

So, from an early age, besides going to school, I had daily chores to do, catechism lessons once a week, church on Sundays, more chores on the weekends, and altogether not nearly enough time to run amok.

It's not that Mom was opposed to pleasure, per se, but it wasn't something she encouraged, either. In her value system, life was something you took seriously, and personal responsibility in particular was non-negotiable.

It was this core value of hers—taking responsibility for oneself and one's actions—that I remember above all others, because Mom never once let it slip by. Throughout my childhood the quickest way to get into real trouble was to try to weasel out of a problem or situation by blaming someone or something else. To Mom's everlasting credit, it may well have been the single most valuable thing I ever learned, and the first lesson I remember began with a broken glass.

Shortly after moving into our new house in Arroyo Grande, I was helping Mom with the laundry. Normally my job consisted only of placing my dirty clothes in the hamper and, later, putting my clean clothes in their proper drawers, but on this particular Saturday morning I was helping bring all the dirty laundry out to the garage. There, Mom sorted it into three different piles: whites, colors, and

---

32 Beginning with weekly catechism lessons and continuing with Catholic grammar school and Catholic high school, Mom strove to ensure that all her children would devoutly follow in that faith. A noble crusade to be sure (and, perhaps, not without some moral benefit), but, in the end, I'm afraid, dreadfully unsuccessful.

delicates—all of which were then divided into smaller piles reflective of the washing machine's capacity.

I couldn't actually see the top of the washing machine, but, by standing on my tiptoes, I could reach just far enough over my head to open the lid. Unfortunately, someone had placed a glass jar on top of the washing machine—a place I couldn't see—and, when I opened the lid on the washing machine, the glass jar went flying through the air and onto the concrete floor—instantly shattering into countless tiny pieces.

Complete silence followed as Mom looked up from her sorting, realized what had happened and then stared directly at me. To her unspoken question I responded as innocently as possible, "The glass broke."

Mom waited for a moment, then, with a surprisingly calm but steely conviction, replied, "No."

Really? I thought to myself in utter confusion. (I'd seen broken glass before, and I was pretty sure this particular glass jar was about as broken as it could get.)

Sensing my bewilderment, Mom tried again. "You broke the glass."

Okay, I thought to myself, we're getting somewhere, and then responded in agreement, "Right, the glass broke."

Mom paused, looked at me again and slowly said, "No, *you* broke the glass."

I still didn't get it. We both seemed to agree there was broken glass in the garage, but for some crazy reason Mom kept repeating my sentences. Realizing that I was never going to resolve this *Paradox of the Pronouns*, she walked over to me and, in a voice that I still remember as being stern rather than angry, began to explain: "Mike, the glass didn't break all by itself. *You* broke the glass, and when something like that happens you need to take responsibility for it and say '*I* broke the glass.' So, get a broom and clean this up."

It would be very nice to conclude this chapter with something like, "*At that very instant the clouds parted, a beam of light burst forth, and in a moment of perfect clarity I understood all that Mom wanted to teach me regarding personal responsibility.*"

In truth, nothing even remotely resembling that imagined ending ever occurred, and I'm afraid Mom would feel it necessary to repeat variations of this lesson with more frequency than I care to recall. Whether it was spilled milk, missing homework assignments, or a broken window—whatever the problem caused by my action or inaction—Mom's position was always the same: there had better be an "*I*" in my opening sentence.

CHAPTER 27

The Cold War

For anyone who missed the 1960s (which today is most everyone) it's easy to look back wistfully at that decade when "Rock and Roll" was king and the modern-day perils of social media, fake news (both real and imagined), and COVID weren't just unknown, they were unimagined. But don't fool yourself. The lack of all those modern-day problems were more than offset by the realities faced by those of us who lived through that insanely crazy period.

It was a decade that began with the promise of John F Kennedy[33] and ended with the accomplishment of America landing a man on the moon, but between those proud bookends were a series of domestic riots, political assassinations, racially motivated bombings, anti-war protests, nuclear brinkmanship, the Vietnam War, and much more.

It's a list well beyond the scope of our story, but the mayhem within that decade left a lasting impression on our narrator. Indeed,

---

33 At age 43 JFK was the youngest president ever elected. Though he won the popular election against Richard Nixon by just 112,827 votes (or 0.17%) JFK went on to enjoy a 70%+ approval rating—the highest of any sitting President since polling began in 1937.

the 60's encompassed my most formative years (ages 7-17) and that experience, in combination with the people I grew up with, goes a long way in explaining why I emerged from this period with the unshakable conviction that the world, along with a great many people who inhabit it, are far stranger than is generally assumed ...and nothing better illustrates this belief than the prescription-strength combination of terror and stupidity produced by the Cold War.

Fought between the USA and the USSR (and in a broader sense between capitalism and communism), the Cold War began shortly after World War II as both sides sought to remake the post-war world in their own image. Mercifully, the two superpowers did manage to avoid direct conflict (i.e. a "hot" war). Instead, and for the next 40 years, they contented themselves with a series of proxy wars across the globe because neither side could ever figure out how to stop fighting.

Even today, with the gift of 20-20 hindsight, it's not clear what might have stopped all this state-sponsored stupidity, but in the early 1960's policymakers could only see a short list of poor choices. So, opting for their "least, worst, bad idea" they instituted a strategy known as MAD (Mutual Assured Destruction).[34]

It was an idea just as dreadful as the acronym suggests and, as the concept of MAD became ever more understood, the general public became ever more terrified. However, rather than question the sanity of MAD, policymakers concluded that the real problem lay not in its substance but rather in the public's perception.

---

34 Perhaps the finest acronym ever devised, MAD posited that an attacking nuclear-armed adversary could, in a sneak attack, destroy its opponent. However, enough of the opponent's nuclear arsenal would survive to assure the aggressor's destruction in a retaliatory strike.

Thus began the short-lived Office of Civil Defense, whose mission was to persuade the average American that a nuclear war with the Russians wouldn't be all that bad. Indeed, surviving a thermonuclear bomb (H-bomb) was so easy even a seven-year-old could do it.

In 1960, I was one of those seven-year-olds.

I was in the second-grade (attending my third school) and part of our curriculum was a short film provided by the Office of Civil Defense with the title, *Duck and Cover*. Shown to millions of elementary school children across America, the film starred two high school students, Paul and Patty, who calmly demonstrated to viewers that, if we noticed a brilliant flash of light (i.e. an exploding H-Bomb), all we had to do to save ourselves was: duck under our desks; curl up in a ball; and cover our head with our hands.

Seemingly alone among my fellow classmates, I recognized immediately that Paul and Patty were deranged.

You see, Arroyo Grande lies a bit less than 20 miles north of Vandenberg Air Force Base (VAB), and throughout the early 1960's scores of Minute Man Missiles were being test-launched from VAB out over the Pacific Ocean. Shrouded in secrecy, the launches were always a surprise and a special delight to anyone in our community who happened to be looking south. You could actually see the flames from the rocket engine in the first few seconds, which soon turned into a contrail growing ever longer as the missile raced skyward. Even more impressive, however, was the sound, which arrived several seconds later and was so powerful it made your chest vibrate.

Naturally, these frequent and awe-inspiring displays captivated my seven-year-old attention, and, to my eagerly asked questions, Dad began by explaining that the Minute Man Missiles were part of our defense against a Russian attack.

This, of course, is where he should have stopped talking, but Dad, who never would grasp the concept of age-appropriate conversation, was just getting warmed-up. Soon he was explaining why VAB was a high priority target for Russia's long-range bombers and missiles, how deadly radioactive fallout could be, and (what I remember most of all) Russia's new 50-megaton H-Bomb, which would obliterate everything within 30 miles.

Even as a seven-year-old I could do that math—we were *inside* the obliteration zone—so, unless Paul and Patty were supplying desks with magic force-fields, I was pretty sure their *Duck and Cover* advice wasn't going to save me from a nuclear fireball hotter than the sun.

Yet, faced with the real and growing possibility of nuclear war, most everyone (including Dad) chose to ignore that existential threat. Instead, they went on with their lives with all the normality they could muster, and I was happy to follow along ... until late October 1962.

By then I was 10 years old, we were living in house number six, and I had just arrived home from (another new) school when Dad rushed in through the front door. This was unusual. Dad never came home from work early, but that was nothing compared to his next move, which was to begin filling the bathtub.

As far as I knew my father had never taken a bath in his life and to my startled inquiry as to what had prompted these sudden behavioral changes, he began to explain the Cuban Missile Crisis.

As usual, Dad went on for some length, but the short version was that the U.S. and the Russians were playing nuclear brinkmanship and within the next few hours either the Russians would back down, or we would be at war. The water in the bathtub, Dad explained, would be for drinking in case we were attacked.

Looking up at my Dad, and then back down at the slowly filling bathtub, I can still remember thinking to myself, "Oh man, we are sooooo screwed!"

Had Dad forgotten about the obliteration zone? Did he not remember how hot a nuclear fireball was? What we needed was a fast car, a full tank of gas, and reservations for any place that was hundreds of miles away from ground zero. But, as useless as Dad's plan appeared on the surface, it was actually much worse, because—having never used the bathtub he was now filling—Dad was unaware that it had a slow leak, which meant that the entirety of his plan to save the family would literally be down the drain in about 10 minutes.

My grandfather's response was a bit more deliberate.

Convinced that the Cuban Missile Crisis wasn't an anomaly, Abe spent the next few months directing the construction of a steel reinforced concrete bomb shelter that would have survived anything short of a direct hit by a nuclear-tipped ICBM. It was also huge (by bomb shelter standards), measuring almost 1,000 square feet with connecting underground fuel and water tanks, a state-of-the-art air filtration system, and enough food to last several families for a month. To the relief of all humanity, Abe's bomb shelter was never used, but it was remarkably illustrative of two conditions:

First, it remains a shining example of Abe's single-minded determination. Once he made up his mind to do something, Abe charged ahead. To be sure, he wasn't always right, but the man never

Abe's bomb shelter under construction. Note pack of cigarettes in foreground to show how closely spaced the steel rebar was in the one-foot thick concrete roof. (Twelve years later Abe would die not from incoming ICBM's but from lung cancer.).

lacked the courage of his convictions.

Second, (and this is the scary part) history would confirm Abe's fear that luck had been just as important as skillful diplomacy in ending the Cuban Missile Crisis. Indeed, the very statesmen (the best and the brightest Kennedy could find) who were credited with avoiding nuclear Armageddon in Cuba would next turn their attention to Southeast Asia.

There, faced with a new variation of the Cold War problem (and blinded by the hubris found only in brilliant minds) they would craft a strategy that led directly to the Vietnam War—the greatest military disaster in our nation's history.

CHAPTER 28

Abe, Version 2.0

To anyone who has followed Abe's story thus far, it should come as little wonder that he was something of a loner. As a rule, he didn't like groups of any kind, never joined any social clubs, and generally preferred his own company. Tragically, that temperament, combined with the stress of his various businesses, along with a likely predisposition to addiction, produced in Abe a severe case of alcoholism that began in early adulthood. His one rule was that he never drank at work. Instead, he typically began drinking after 5 p.m. (the close of business) and would continue steadily until he was completely intoxicated. Usually this took the entire evening, but on particularly bad nights he might consume a pint of bourbon within an hour and then pass out at the dinner table.

Not surprisingly, Abe didn't have a lot of friends. In fact, in his later life he only had one, which to the amazement of most everyone turned out to be Grampy. Although different in nearly every respect, they had found common ground in three shared passions: family was important, fishing was their favorite pastime, and becoming a grandfather was the best thing that had ever happened to either of them.

Unfortunately, once the Miner Family moved to the Central Coast, the only time Abe and Grampy were likely to see one another was at family get-togethers. At these gatherings—birthdays, anniversaries, holidays, and the like—they were able to catch up on recent events, share old stories, and, on rare occasions, disappear altogether to go fishing.

It was just this circumstance—an afternoon fishing trip in 1960—in which something quite extraordinary took place, and when Abe returned home that day, he asked Bee to make him a sandwich.

To the outside observer, an afternoon snack would hardly seem noteworthy, but for Bee it broke a decades-long pattern. Always in the past if Abe arrived home late in the day on a weekend, it meant a tumbler full of bourbon. But not that day. Whatever transpired between Grampy and Abe on that fishing trip remains a mystery (neither of them would ever talk about it), but Abe had made up his mind to quit drinking. In his typical single-minded determination, he quit "cold turkey"—without therapy, without drugs, without support (other than ever-supportive Bee), and without even telling anyone. He never drank again—an accomplishment most experts on addiction hold to be impossible. The next year, just as abruptly and with the same success, he quit smoking.

At age 59—through a combination of hard work, remarkable determination, and a sprinkling of luck—Abe found himself holding three life-changing cards. He was financially independent; he was a new grandfather; and he had defeated alcoholism. The stage was set for the "Mother of All Second Chances," and Abe, who always knew an opportunity when he saw it, seized this one with authority.

Not to overstate his transformation (Abe remained the same gruff, solitary, and no-nonsense kind of guy he always was), but there was a noteworthy shift in his values and focus. With business and alcohol no longer occupying the center of his existence, the world became a much bigger place. Suddenly, there was enough room in his life for self-exploration, for engaging with a generation of grandchildren, and for building a legacy. Until his death some 12 years later, Abe turned his attention to all three.

Sadly, with regard to his relationship with his two sons, Abe's efforts would prove too late and too insufficient to overcome the decades of ugly baggage that already existed between them. For his grandchildren, however, all we ever knew was the new and improved version.

So rather than seeing a man who was either consumed by work or alcohol, his grandchildren experienced, instead, a man who was both available and engaged. This isn't meant to suggest that Abe started acting like Grampy—that persona just wasn't available to him—but within the limits of his personality, Abe did become a remarkable grandfather.

Arguably, it was his greatest accomplishment, and Abe deserves accolades by the bushel-full for all he did to make that happen, but behind the scenes stood Bee.

Throughout their married life, Bee seemed comfortable following Abe's lead, but when it came to their grandchildren, their relationship was different. Try as he might, Abe was just plain awkward around children. He wanted to engage; he just didn't know how. Bee, on the other hand, was like a fairy godmother—a wave of her magic wand and every child within her gaze wanted to get a hug. But the real magic was Bee's ability to gently lead from behind. More than Abe ever realized, she was his guide and mentor during all their grandparenting years.

CHAPTER 29

Abe's Hobby Years

Entrepreneurially speaking, Abe's life from his late 50s to his late 60s was odd, even by his standards. Perhaps it was his version of a sabbatical, but whatever drove the business side of Abe's psyche seemed to have shifted. Gone were the days when profit was the only thing that mattered. (Which is not to suggest that profit was no longer important—Abe *always* liked making money.) Instead, there were other aspects of business that competed for his attention. Indeed, he seems to have entered a phase in which business became almost a hobby.

It began with what might best be described as his "Eccentric Inventor Period" wherein Abe, whose formal education had ended in the eighth grade, began doing chemistry experiments.

The Kolor-Kote debacle from the late 1930s had always haunted him. Abe hated losing under any conditions, especially if it involved money or control. Kolor-Kote represented both. So, after holding on to that grudge for three decades, Abe committed to figuring out the secret formula and recreating the company.

His initial chemistry experiments quickly outgrew the kitchen sink, and in 1959 Abe constructed a small building (known as the Shop) behind Miner's Hardware in Grover Beach—a place he and Bee would call home for the next two years.

From the outside it was about the size and shape of a medium-sized house, but the illusion quickly faded as one got closer. There were almost no windows, and once past the front door, the interior looked like something you might see if you were Superman and had X-ray vision.

At least that's what I imagined during kindergarten and first grade, when I was a frequent after-school visitor.[35] The floor was bare concrete, the exterior walls and ceiling were unfinished and there were no interior walls at all (except for a small bathroom in one corner). Lighting was provided by an assortment of bare incandescent light bulbs hanging from the ceiling, and the heating system consisted of a single portable electrical heater. Actually, the bathroom had heat, or at least it was generally warm there, because that's where the exposed gas water heater lived.

Yet, even with all that was missing, one could still recognize the layout of a home. On the west end of the building was the "garage." There, Abe parked his car and kept a few tools. The "bedroom" was next—a double bed placed atop a small area rug—while in between stood a "wall" of ever-changing boxes and 55-gallon drums all filled

---

35 During kindergarten and first grade, my school, Grover Elementary, was only two blocks away, and Bee, who at this time was typically working in the Shop or helping out next door at Miner's Hardware, often took care of me until Mom picked me up later in the day.

with various chemicals and supplies. Finally, between the front door and the corner bathroom was the "kitchen" (and sometimes laboratory), which consisted of a large concrete double sink next to a tabletop three burner gas stove. The rest of the space was crowded with a confusing assortment of boilers, mixers, pipes, hoses and wires which, when combined with the parked car, managed to infuse the Shop with an air of industriousness—meaning the place smelled like a petroleum plant.

Interestingly, none of this ever struck me as unusual. Partially, this was due to my limited frame of reference: didn't half of all grandparents live in unfinished would-be laboratories? But mostly it didn't seem odd because nobody in my immediate family thought it was odd, which isn't all that surprising when you consider that Dad came of age in a desert mining camp, while his brother, Glenn, being five years younger, spent most of his adolescence living in a small apartment atop the hardware store in Culver City. In the Miner Family, living where you worked (and I mean *exactly* where you worked) was pretty normal stuff.

Anyway, after months of frustration and failed experiments, Abe finally succeeded in reproducing a version of Kolor-Kote that was just as effective as the original.[36]

Unfortunately, for the first and only time, he failed to correctly read the market. The years between the original Kolor-Kote of the

---

36 Apparently, Abe knew that carnauba wax was the "secret" ingredient in Kolor-Kote. The problem was that pure carnauba wax is about as hard as a rock. Somehow, he needed to change it into a creamy paste, which could then be easily applied. Abe eventually discovered that a small amount of eucalyptus oil mixed in with the carnauba wax at just the right temperature solved the problem.

1930s and Abe's successful reformulation in the early 1960s had seen vast improvements in automobile paint technology and there was little demand for the product. He did have some limited success with a high-quality car wax called *Formula 29* and an appliance wax called *Hit*, with both products garnering a small but devoted following. Nevertheless, the venture never turned a profit, and he soon sold the business, equipment, and formulas to a manufacturer in the LA area.

Once again, he decided to retire—this time to the large three-bedroom home he'd just had built a few blocks away in what was then the upscale neighborhood of Grover Heights. This was the house where the cookie jar lived, and where Bee cooked an unreasonable number of meals on Saturday nights. It was also the place where Abe started his worm farm.

How he got interested in worms or learned about their care and feeding remains unknown. Even as a boy I thought it was a bit quirky, although feeding them was pretty interesting. We'd sprinkle kitchen scraps, cornmeal, and old coffee grounds atop each of the 4-foot-by-12-foot raised beds of soil, which Abe had constructed amongst Bee's fruit trees and vegetables. Next (and this was the best part) with each of us using our own garden spade, we'd mix the "food" into the soil. Each turned-over scoop brought hundreds of wiggling (and according to Abe, happy) worms into contact with their next meal. Finally, we'd give them a drink of water by sprinkling each bed with a hose sprayer.

In terms of production, Abe's worm farm soon proved successful. (It turns out that given sufficient resources, earthworms will multiply at a prodigious rate.) However, he hadn't quite figured out the marketing side of his venture, and by the fall of 1962 he was quickly running out of room.

It was a worrisome problem, but just before the worms overtook the entire back yard, the aforementioned Cuban Missile Crisis intervened (see page 192). The worms were released into the wilds of Bee's garden and Abe focused all his energy on the construction of the bomb shelter. A few months later, with the bomb shelter completed and the crisis resolved, he charged ahead in an entirely new direction.

*   *   *   *

For years Abe had been interested in stamps, and by the early 1960s his collection included every U.S. stamp ever printed from the beginning of the U.S. Postal Service in 1775 until just after World War I (along with a smattering of international stamps from various periods and countries). It was massive. There were boxes and catalogs, books and magnifying lamps, special cleaners, special envelopes, and strangest of all (in my boyhood memory), tweezers.

Stamps, it turned out, were not to be touched. They could only be carefully picked up with special tweezers and then carefully stored in special envelopes. The other thing you could do with stamps was to stare at them. That was it: pick them up; move them in and out of special envelopes; and stare at them. That's what you did with stamps.

As a boy I never could get the hang of stamp collecting. It was like having toys you couldn't play with. What was the point? Still, there was something both bizarre and mysterious about the whole process, and on rare occasions, after I solemnly vowed to be *extraordinarily* careful, Abe would let me perform the tweezers-envelope-staring ritual with him.

This didn't happen very often—Abe knew how limited my attention span was at that age—so amongst the thousands of stamps he owned, he tried to show me only the most interesting ones.

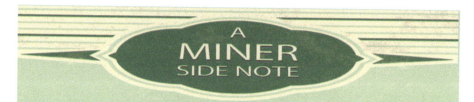

A MINER SIDE NOTE

MINING FOR GOLD

While the coin and stamp business remained a focus for Abe and Bee during the mid-1960s (more or less), they also purchased a travel trailer around this time and briefly became frequent visitors to the Gold Country of California (Grass Valley, the Yuba River, Nevada City, etc.). With their sluice box and gold pans they scoured the various creeks and rivers for gold and actually found a few ounces. Even better, and to Bee's lifelong delight, she unearthed a real gold nugget.

In a story she particularly enjoyed telling, Bee was nearing the end of a long and unfruitful day of prospecting when she deliberately paused, slowly surveyed her surroundings, and quietly asked herself a question.

"If I were a gold nugget, where would I be?"

The answer, she felt, was under an old tree standing nearby. So, after digging several shovelfuls of dirt and gravel from around its base, she began pouring all of it into the sluice box.

"And there it was!" she would proudly explain. Then with a wistful smile, slowly add, "But it only worked once."

His best stamp had its own name, *Cattle in the Storm*. It was the pride of his collection, and Abe kept it in a separate and special envelope. Even promising to be extra careful, I wasn't allowed to participate in the tweezers-envelope portion of the ritual, but Abe once placed it momentarily in my open palm for me to stare at. By itself this was memorable, but when he mentioned that the stamp was worth $500, I was stunned. My Dad's pickup truck wasn't worth $500, and the idea that I was holding that much value in my hand was the craziest, most incomprehensible thing I'd ever experienced.

Yet, as impressive as a $500 postage stamp was, there were two other stamps that I liked even more. One was from the Pony Express and the other from the Civil War. Neither was particularly valuable or attractive, but the idea that I was holding an object (carefully and with tweezers) that had been used a hundred years ago by *real* people— people I had learned about in school—left a lasting impression. For the first time I found myself wondering if history might be more than dates and dead people …

But as interesting as stamp collecting was (or wasn't), its popularity paled when compared to the country's growing fascination with coin collecting. There were a number of reasons for this, but chief among them was that, in the years leading up to and just after World War II, the U.S. Mint had made changes to nearly every coin it produced, the consequence being that the discontinued coins started to become rare and therefore valuable. By the late 1950s and early 1960s, Americans everywhere were searching their pockets, dresser drawers, and old piggy banks for treasure. Indian Head pennies, Buffalo nickels,

Mercury dimes, and more all became collector's items.[37] Suddenly coin clubs began sprouting up across the country, Abe saw an opportunity, and for a few years in the mid-1960s he and Bee ran a small Coin and Stamp Shop.

Taken as a group, Abe's ventures into chemistry, worms, stamps, and more look just like something one might expect to see in the declining years of an old businessman, but in this assumption, one would be very much mistaken. Despite their hobby-like appearance, Abe was still following the same pattern he'd always used: find something interesting and figure out how to make money at it.

True, these businesses were all on a smaller scale, and required less of Abe's attention than previous ventures, but that didn't mean Abe's business acumen was diminishing. Incredibly, and as if to prove this very point, he was saving what was arguably his best business idea of all until the end.

---

37 Abe's coin collection actually surpassed his stamp collection in both breadth and value, and he was particularly proud of his $20 Liberty Head gold coins from the late 1800s. However, as a little boy, the most astonishing coin to me was a very rare penny (1909 SVDB), which looked just like any other penny I'd ever seen but was somehow worth $100 in the 1960s!

CHAPTER 30

Mom's Career

While Dad was immersed in Miner's Hardware, building spec homes, and moving our family from house to house, Mom was working away at her own career goals, and in 1961, after years of juggling motherhood, substitute teaching, and college, she landed her first full-time job at Orchard Elementary School in Arroyo Grande.

She began as a first-grade teacher, moved to second and third grade, and a few years later moved again to middle school, where she taught English and girls' P.E. As a quick aside, Mom's stint as an English teacher made perfect sense—she was something of a grammarian—but teaching girls' P.E. might have been the most incongruent thing she ever did. (In her world ladies never perspired on purpose, and Mom avoided all forms of physical exercise whenever possible—she didn't even like walking.)

Yet, despite her obvious incompatibility with P.E., she continued to get high marks as a teacher. She was generally liked by her students and certainly earned the respect of her fellow teachers. For the rest of her life, she maintained close ties with a handful of colleagues from her years at Orchard Elementary, and at her funeral one of them, in a voice filled with both pride and wistfulness, fondly recalled those early days when they were all young teachers still learning their craft.

Perhaps the most touching tribute to her success as a teacher, though, came from one of her first students: a little boy who had trouble reading. Mom gave him the extra help he needed to succeed and many years later, when she was terminally ill, he was the doctor who remained at the hospital late into the night desperately working to give Mom a few more hours to say goodbye to her family.

By her mid-30s, Mom's career was beginning to take off. Her children were all in school, and her teaching success at Orchard Elementary, along with her master's degree, combined to help her land a coveted new position in the reading department with the San Luis Obispo Unified School District. Here, and for just over a decade, she had the good fortune to work with a handful of talented women, all of whom became lifelong friends. She did groundbreaking work in English as a Second Language (ESL), became head of the new ESL Department, and was hired by the book publisher, Prentice Hall, to produce a textbook on the subject.

All of it was important and exciting work, but the textbook project was by far the most extraordinary. Besides out-of-town meetings in San Francisco, Prentice Hall also flew her to Boston on three separate occasions to collaborate with her fellow ESL authors. Remember, this was the mid-1960s, when only a small percentage of the population had ever seen the inside of an airplane and no one we knew had ever flown cross-country. Even a coast-to-coast phone call was a big deal. It required operators at both ends to literally push individual wire leads into receptacles on a control board in front of them in order to complete the audio circuit. The cost per minute was more than most people's hourly wage. So, when Mom landed in Boston on that first trip and called home to let us know she'd arrived safely, her conversation with Dad lasted less than 60 seconds.

It was a busy time with never enough hours in the day for Mom to do all the things she had tasked herself with, including sleeping—a condition that led to one of the more famous stories within the ESL Department.

Having spent the weekend in Boston, Mom flew home late Sunday night. The next morning, with very little sleep, she drove to one of the outlying schools, where she was scheduled to spend the day meeting with various students and provide one-to-one instruction specific to their needs. So, when her first student was late, Mom decided it would be a good idea to put her head on the desk and rest for a few moments. She fell asleep instantly, and a few minutes later the tardy 6-year-old student arrived to find his teacher unresponsive. The poor kid assumed the worst and ran all the way to the principal's office screaming, "Mrs. Miner's dead! Mrs. Miner's dead!"

This had an immediate effect on the administrative staff, most of whom sprinted across campus and burst into Mom's office. Even their noisy entrance didn't rouse her, and for a moment everyone feared the student's prognosis had been correct. However, after some shaking and shouting by the principal, she returned to consciousness—a relief to everyone except Mom, who nearly died from embarrassment.

*   *   *   *

Her years as head of the ESL department marked the zenith of Mom's career, and she would forever relish both the success and camaraderie she found within that special group of professional women. Unfortunately, it didn't last. In her early 40s the entire department was dismantled due to budget cuts and shifting priorities.

It was a crushing disappointment, and Mom rarely spoke about this new direction in her career—never in any detail. Coming almost full circle, she returned to the classroom and spent the remainder of her career teaching English to middle school students.

CHAPTER 31

The Elephant in the Room

For reasons I've never understood and have long since despaired of ever resolving, the 1960s would see Mom and Dad both descend into alcoholism. Dad, who had begun drinking regularly and heavily at least as far back as his days in the Navy, crossed the line somewhere in the early part of that decade. Mom held out a while longer but eventually followed him down that dark path.

How lives that had held such promise and had begun with such remarkable success could then stumble and lose their way begs an unending series of "why" and "what-if" questions. I have no answers for any of them. Dad died from the disease in his mid-50s, Mom in her early 60s.

In that increasingly dysfunctional environment, Kitty, Steve, and I grew up fast, self-reliant, and with gaping holes in our understanding of human relationships. By age 12 (the earliest the law would allow), I began working summers in the fields harvesting strawberries and green beans. By high school I was dividing my time between school, work, sports, and anything else that would keep me away from home.

At age 17, a week after graduating from high school, I left for good. Kitty and Steve followed similar trajectories.

I wish (with more intensity than I can ever express) that I could write our parents a different story, one with the same promising beginning but with a different middle and ending, one in which, together, they both triumphed against life's hardships and disappointments. Instead, my siblings and I watched helplessly as our parents seemed to career through life—bouncing between behaviors that ranged from impressive to inexcusable, from redeeming to ruinous, from heartfelt to heartbreaking.

From a child's perspective, nothing good can be said of parental alcoholism or its effects. It doesn't provide any insights; it isn't character-building; it's never funny. Home becomes a place that isn't safe; a place that isn't kind; a place where bad memories don't just overwhelm the good—they all but obliterate them.

And yet...as accurate and damning as these last few paragraphs remain, with every passing year I'm less sure they're fair. With that thought in mind, it's worth making two observations.

First, the power of alcohol remains a mystery to me. For this I get no credit—moral or otherwise. By a chance shuffling of genetic code, my body has always considered a blood alcohol level that even begins to approach intoxication as proof that I've been poisoned, and only an epic response from my stomach (and I'm pretty sure several feet of my upper intestines) will save me. By age 22, after three or four valiant attempts, I gave up entirely on ever getting drunk. To this day, a beer or two is all my constitution has ever allowed.

Second, (and more importantly) Mom and Dad weren't always drunk. Their professional lives mostly held together, and there were times—surely more than I can credit them for—when they rose to the occasion and acted like the parents they wanted to be. Sadly, my memories contain only a few examples, but of those events two in particular stand out and, oddly, both are connected to the War in Vietnam.

It was the beginning of my sophomore year in high school. I had just turned 15 and, like most 15-year-olds, I was all but oblivious to global events. However, as I concentrated on basketball, struggled with geometry, and became increasingly mystified by girls, halfway around the world a thousand young American soldiers were being killed each month in Vietnam.

Relatively speaking this was still early in the conflict and most Americans were still supportive of the Vietnam War—convinced of both its righteousness and ultimate victory—but Mom was growing increasingly worried. Having lived through World War II and the Korean Conflict, she knew all too well that wars didn't have end dates and that in less than three years her first child could be drafted into the U.S. Army.

It was a prospect that worried her more than I ever knew and in September of 1967 something quite unexpected happened. It was an otherwise typical day and Mom was driving home from her teaching job in San Luis Obispo. A regular listener of KVEC (the local news radio station) she tuned in just as they got to the segment covering local young men who had been killed in Vietnam that day. Often there were no names at all. Occasionally there could be three or four, but on this day there was only one: Michael Miner.[38]

This produced a rather strong and visceral response from Mom, who, upon arriving home, ran into the house and started hugging and kissing me. For several minutes I thought she'd lost her mind.

Tragically, stupidly, futilely, senselessly (the list of negative adverbs is utterly inadequate) the war in Vietnam would continue, and by early August of 1971, at age 18, I became eligible for the draft.[39] As a college student I had escaped the previous year, but now those deferments had been withdrawn, and in a few days a new lottery system would determine my fate.

Unexpectedly and unknown to me, Dad was nearly as conflicted and frightened during this period as I was. The death toll in Vietnam by now exceeded more than 50,000 American lives, and Dad's value system—formed as a proud World War II veteran—was being shaken to its core.

This led to a decision on his part that can only be appreciated in context, because in Dad's world the end of any of his children's high school days marked the end of his parental responsibilities. This particularly applied to financial support and, by the time my number was about to be drawn in the lottery, I had been on my own (including paying for college) for more than a year. It therefore came as complete surprise when Dad tracked me down and offered to support me if I

---

38 An 18 year-old boy from San Luis Obispo High School.

39 The last U.S. combat troops left on March 29, 1973, after 58,220 (mostly young men) had died.

decided to escape the draft by fleeing to Canada (an option we'd never discussed and one I hadn't seriously considered).

In the end luck was on my side. My birthdate drew a high lottery number, which meant that I was forever free from the draft, and even though I've always suspected Dad's definition of "support" involved a loan I'd have to repay, his offer was sincere and every bit as surprising as Mom's hugs and kisses from a few years earlier.

CHAPTER 32

The '70s

Historians sometimes refer to the 1970s as a "pivot of change" which is polite history-talk for "nothing much happened." I mean, really, other than the release of *Star Wars* in 1977 (which was epic), the decade's most lasting cultural contribution was probably the Lava Lamp.

Yet, as unmemorable as the 1970s were on the national scale, they were entirely consequential in my world.

After leaving home at the end of high school in the summer of 1970, I spent the next year and a half at UC Davis and Cal Poly. Academically, I did well, but after four quarters I'd spent all the money saved from working during high school, and the prospect of accumulating a pile of student debt to attend classes that seemed of little practical value led to my dropping out just after my 19th birthday.

And then, of course, there was Susie.

Although we'd known each other since the sixth grade, we hadn't started dating until halfway through our senior year of high school. College saw each of us briefly head in different directions, but when

I transferred back to nearby Cal Poly in 1971, our relationship became serious. On March 11, 1972, we got married.

There are a hundred reasons why getting married at age 19 is problematic, and we ran headlong into our share of them. Yet, in the end, it worked. (As I write this, we're approaching our 53rd Anniversary.) That said, we'll both readily admit that those first years were tough—especially the economic part.

I was bouncing from job to job building and remodeling houses while Susie bounced between working and going to school to become a Registered Nurse (she graduated and passed the state exam in 1977). For the two of us it was a mix of adventure and anxiety, and though it's satisfying to look back on our (mostly) successful navigation of that period, I can tell you that neither of us wants to do it again.

There was, however, one aspect of being young and inexperienced that's worth remembering: you have no idea what's not possible.

So, for example, I was unaware of how complicated it would be to remove, rebuild, and replace the engine in my work truck, and Susie and I had even less appreciation for the difficulties we would face in enlarging and remodeling the house we purchased in 1972 (a 1930s era seller-financed dwelling that should have been condemned). It also came as a complete shock that banks had rules against approving home-improvement loans to 20-year-olds with no assets.

Today, with the "wisdom" of old age, we both know better than to attempt any of the above, but in our early 20s we were fearless (-ly dumb) and forged ahead with enthusiasm and the following results:

- Rebuilding a truck engine requires numerous critical steps and I got all of them right except one … which turned out to be fatal. Mortifyingly—after all my work—the truck had to be towed to a real mechanic.

- While ultimately completed, our first house proved to be in such dismal condition that it took five years and thousands of hours of working nights and weekends to finish.

- After the first banker politely explained, "I would lose my job if I gave you a loan," we had no better success with the second banker. However, I finally convinced banker #3 to lend us about 60% of what we actually needed to finish the house even as he stated, "the loan committee is not going to like this."

I should mention here—from the safe perspective of nearly 50 years—that looking back on these examples (and others like them) always makes me smile twice: first, for the tenacity displayed by our younger selves, and second (the bigger smile) because we're not there anymore.

Meanwhile, as Susie and I struggled through our early 20s, the rest of the Miner Family was busily engaged in their own pursuits. To wit, in the early part of the 1970s, if one had taken a leisurely drive down Grand Avenue (the commercial corridor that joins Arroyo Grande with Grover Beach) one might have noticed three similarly named businesses: Miner's Home Appliance, Miner's Hardware, and Miner's Antiques. They were owned, respectively, by my father, uncle, and grandfather.

In the Miner Family, running your own business is what we did. At least that's how it must have felt to me, when, at age twenty-two, I began to follow a similar path. My new career choice would see its share of challenge, success, and (to the benefit of our story) the kind of daily interaction with most of the characters in this book that only a family business can provide.

*   *   *   *

In 1974, in a move that even now surprises me, I accepted an offer to join my father's appliance business—selling and repairing washing machines, refrigerators, TVs, etc. It had been five years since I'd left home and in that time much had changed between me and Dad. There were a multitude of reasons for this (and my being 22 instead of 17 was among them), but the bigger factor was that Dad proved to be a much better businessman than he ever was a father. Just as surprisingly, I quickly displayed a much greater talent for business that anyone had suspected (especially me).

Sales began to rise, profits increased, and before the end of my second year Dad offered me a chance to purchase half the business—an opportunity I accepted but didn't fully appreciate at the time. By year four in my new career Miner's Home Appliance was on a roll. Sales had doubled over the previous year and we were becoming a real powerhouse—by local standards, anyway.

It was all very exciting and, while I'd like to take *all* the credit for our retail success, rapidly improving technology did help a bit.

I know, it's hard to believe that technology was even a thing back in the '70s—especially when the decade began with the *World's Smallest*

Handheld Calculator. This "luggable" four-function calculator weighed nearly four pounds and sold for $495—a whopping $4,000 in 2024 dollars!

Still, it was impressive for its day and an outstanding example of "Moore's Law"[40]— by the end of the decade Sharp's newest calculator was the size of a credit card and sold for $34.95 ($150 in 2024 dollars).

However, the most far-reaching (pun intended) technological achievement of the decade was the Voyager 1 and Voyager 2 Spacecrafts.[41] Launched in 1977, they flew by (and sent back detailed pictures and data

Introduced in 1970 by Sharp Electronics, the QT-8B sold for $495.

of) Jupiter, Saturn, Uranus, and Neptune. Even now they continue to impress: traveling 35,000 mph away from Earth they remain the fastest human-made objects ever built; the only human-made objects ever to leave our Solar System; and, incredibly, they're both still sending back information.

But for all the Voyager Mission accomplishments perhaps the most extraordinary information they returned happened some 13

---

40 In 1965, Gordon Moore, then CEO of Intel, posited that roughly every two years, the number of transistors on microchips would double and the price of computers will be halved. More than 50 years later "Moore's Law" is still working.

41 The Voyager missions are extraordinary by any measure and even more so considering the "advanced" technology of their day. By way of comparison, if your current cell phone was using Voyager technology, you'd need to carry it in a suitcase, conversations would only be in text, and its entire memory would be filled by a single picture.

years after launch. Flying past Neptune—the last planet on its journey out of our Solar System—Voyager 1 was heading into interstellar space and struggling to remain operational. Half of its instruments had been turned off to save power, but, with enough energy remaining for one final picture, Mission Control instructed Voyager to turn its camera toward Earth (then almost 4 billion miles away). Barely visible in the frame was a pale blue dot—less than a pixel in size—which inspired Carl Sagan to write this beautiful and compelling appeal to humanity:

> Look again at that dot. That's here. That's home. That's us. On it everyone you love, everyone you know, everyone you ever heard of, every human being who ever was, lived out their lives...
>
> Our posturings, our imagined self-importance, the delusion that we have some privileged position in the universe, are challenged by this point of pale light...

As an aside, I encourage the Gentle Reader to lookup Sagan's *Pale Blue Dot* and read it in its entirety. It's a thought-provoking piece that always leaves me wondering how much better the world might be if, rather than Pledging Allegiance to 195 different nation-states and vastly more religions, humanity, instead, remembered that tiny spec of light—that pale blue dot—and said together, **"That's here. That's home. That's us."**

*   *   *   *

Back on Earth all this new and improving technology was producing a host of new and never-before-seen consumer products such as:

VCRs, digital watches, video games, portable cassette players, and (to the good fortune of the home appliance business) the Microwave Oven.

Discovered by accident clear back in World War II (while researchers were working on Radar) the appliance industry couldn't quite figure out what to do with the idea. They completely bungled a 1955 introduction with a microwave oven that cost almost as much as a new automobile and didn't do much better in 1967 with the introduction of the "Radarange"—a name that should have gotten everyone in the Marketing Department fired. (Understandably, not many people were keen on having Radar in their kitchen.)

However, all that changed by the mid-1970s when microwave ovens became both affordable and user-friendly. Happily, Miner's Home Appliance found itself in much the same situation that Abe had enjoyed with his truckload of galvanized products back in 1946—demand was outpacing supply. For most of 1975 and 1976 I could sell every microwave oven I could get my hands on (and I managed to lay hands on a few hundred).

Yet, despite our growing success I found myself enjoying the appliance business less and less. Competition was brutal, suppliers were often untrustworthy, and very few customers enjoyed spending a month's take-home pay for most of the items we sold—the repair side of the business was no fun at all. By the beginning of year five I wanted out. But before we venture down that road, our story must first return to my grandfathers.

CHAPTER 33

Abe's Grand Finale

I n the late 1960s, while I was absorbed in all the passages of high school, much of the West Coast was becoming fascinated with antique furniture (roughly defined as being made before 1910). Perhaps it was a response to the social turbulence of the '60s, wherein antiques symbolized simpler times and traditional values, or maybe it was a newfound appreciation for the beauty and craftsmanship of an era before mass production, but whatever the cause, demand far exceeded supply.

The reason for this was simple: before 1910 very few furniture makers lived west of the Mississippi. Indeed, not many people of any persuasion lived west of the Mississippi before 1910, and of those who did, most had chosen careers in areas such as farming, ranching, and gold mining.

Interestingly, this was not the situation on the East Coast, where, particularly in the New England states, craftsmen had been making fine furniture since the 1700s.

Here was a problem Abe had been born to solve, and in 1969, at age 67, he and Bee headed to Maine. It was early spring and, with patches of snow still on the ground, they began visiting small towns, old barns, and estate sales.

Seemingly everywhere they looked, antique furniture was for sale, and in less than a month Abe and Bee had filled a temporary warehouse with dressers, sideboards, armoires, tables, and an assortment of lamps, clocks, and the like. These were then shipped back to Grover Beach, where Abe had rented a large and long-vacant building on Grand Avenue.

By early summer Miner's Antiques was open for business, and in just over three months, everything had been sold. It was a success that caught even Abe by surprise, and for a short time he struggled with indecision—neither he nor Bee wanted the stress and obligation of another full-time business.

So, in a solution nearly as brilliant as the business itself, they decided to close the store six months each year. Fall and winter were vacation and family time, but by late March they were back in New England, where an ever-growing number of brokers and dealers awaited their arrival. Purchases were stepped up, and, to further increase supply, carpenters and craftsmen were hired to make repairs and restorations on damaged and over-used antiques.

Each Memorial Day weekend, Miner's Antiques would re-open for the season and close again in early October. Hours were short (Friday through Sunday 10-5), their lines of supply secured (and secret); and profits were rising every year.

It was like living in retail heaven.

CHAPTER 34

The End of an Era

By his early '70s, Abe, who had enjoyed robust health his entire life, began to decline. He ignored the symptoms for nearly a year before finally seeing a doctor. It was lung cancer. Treatment options were discussed, but Abe didn't like the odds. He'd seen too many people suffer needlessly through chemotherapy and radiation treatments and declined any intervention.

I was in my very early 20s at this point, and Abe's sudden death sentence felt *wrong* in a way the world had never felt wrong before. Along with Grampy, Abe was the most important man in my life, and (though it took me some time to recognize it) I was terrified at the thought of his absence. There must be a way to fix this, I kept thinking, but even in those first few days—at the peak of my denial—I knew he was leaving.

My solution was to grab on to what little life Abe had left—almost literally. I had regularly visited Abe and Bee my entire life. Now, and for the rest of Abe's illness, I began to visit them in earnest.

Until his death six months later—almost exactly the time his doctor had guessed—I would stop at Abe's and Bee's house every weekday morning on my way to work. Susie often joined me on the weekend, but typically, it was just me and my grandparents.[42] Those visits varied somewhat as Abe's illness progressed, but generally I'd arrive about 7 a.m., spend 15 minutes or so sharing a cup of coffee with Abe in the living room, and then another 15 minutes alone with Bee in the kitchen over a quick breakfast. It was a routine that soon became the best part of my day and even towards the end, when Abe became very ill and conversation increasingly difficult, I still looked forward to those daily visits.

Those months turned out to be among the strangest and most powerful of my entire life. Powerful, because of all that Abe taught me about dying. Strange, because even as Abe's condition deteriorated and his death drew ever closer, there was still joy in their house. In every sense, "It was the best of times; it was the worst of times"—and I can tell you there is hard truth in that famous and pithy quote from Dickens.

It was the worst of times because, as a very young man with little experience and less wisdom, I could see death only as a frightening horror. Even more distressing was the helplessness I felt as Abe's cancer slowly devoured him. From a robust (if somewhat overweight) 180 pounds, he would lose almost half his body weight before the end. From a purely physical experience, everything about his dying was appalling.

---

42 Shortly after Susie and I started dating, I introduced her to Abe and Bee. Bee liked her immediately but that was hardly unusual–Bee liked everybody. Abe, however, was charmed well beyond my expectations and had a soft spot in his heart for her ever since.

However, it was also the best of times, because Abe's unique view of the world allowed him to face death with a combination of courage and peace that I've rarely seen equaled. He wasn't focused on his physical decay; he was focused on his mental attitude, and in those last months he was never afraid and never angry.

*   *   *   *

Only months after Abe's death, in the autumn of 1974, Grampy, who had been in poor health for most of the previous year, began to rapidly decline. His heart, already damaged by two previous heart attacks, along with his smoking, poor diet, and lack of exercise, all contributed to a fatal prognosis.

It was shocking news, and yet, because it lacked the definitive diagnosis and timetable of lung cancer, everyone in the family tried to ignore it. Maybe the doctors were wrong …

They weren't. Grampy got steadily worse, and as the year drew to a close, everyone within the immediate family who had made other plans for the holidays changed them in order to be at Grammie and Grampy's house.

By Christmas Eve we'd all arrived. Throughout the house Christmas displays adorned every tabletop and doorway, and in the living room stood a perfect Christmas tree—decorated with the same big frilly ornaments and the same lights Grammie had used since the first Christmas any of us could remember. Underneath were stacks of presents, and the smell of Christmas cookies—jubilee jumbles, sugar cookies, and Mexican wedding cake cookies—filled the air. It was a scene right out of a Norman Rockwell painting.

The next morning, we all gathered around the tree and began to open presents, while Grampy, bundled up in blankets and sitting as comfortably as his condition would allow, looked on. He was thin, pale, and breathing with some difficulty. From the outside he looked as ill as he probably felt, and everyone knew he'd never be part of this ritual again.

But the twinkle in his eye told us all not to worry. He was here on *this* morning and that was all that mattered. Surrounded by the people he treasured most in the world, Grampy was as happy as any of us have ever seen him.

As the festivities of the morning continued, I watched his gaze move slowly around the room, landing on each person in turn.

At each stop he'd pause, as though replaying a hundred special memories. Finally, it was my turn. Our eyes met and in that moment we were fishing at Lake Cachuma, loading the back seat of his car with newspapers, and riding the raft to Tom Sawyer's Island. More recent memories added to the mix, but the best part was that within his gaze I knew he was exaggerating me. Just as he had with everyone else in their turn, Grampy's expression told me that he was looking at the best and most interesting person he'd ever known. It was his final gift and as nice a thing as anyone has ever said to me.

Grampy passed away on January 10, 1975.

In the span of just a few months, the two most important men in my life had both died. It was the end an era, and for a long time the world didn't seem very full.

A
MINER
SIDE NOTE

FROM THE *LOS ANGELES TIMES,* JANUARY 21, 1975

Those widows who have eagerly looked forward to getting that heart-shaped box of chocolates on Valentine's Day for a number of years will not get it this year. The kind person who had deep compassion for the lonely and depressed died January 10 of a heart condition. He was Jim Newton.

It was some years before recipients of the Valentine remembrance found out who the kind Samaritan was who remembered them on sweetheart day. It was a most delightful surprise to find the bright red box at one's doorstep.

Some of the recipients were in convalescent homes, some widows of former dear friends of Jim and some lonely people. Valentine's Day this year will be a sad day of memories for this good kind man, a Rotarian, a fourth-degree knight of the Knights of Columbus, an esteemed Elk and a friend to everyone.

CHAPTER 35

The Lessons of My Grandfathers

Despite how grievous the death of my grandfathers felt at the time, life went on—pulling the living in new directions and offering new challenges. Babies were born, loan payments came due, friends got married, and (to my great surprise) my own life soon filled with new people and new opportunities.

Yet, even as my grief subsided, I found myself returning again and again to the memories of my grandfathers. What counsel would they have given? What lessons would they have shared? What made them tick?

With time and experience I would gradually begin to answer those rhetorical questions, but it was a slow process—one made all the more difficult because of how extraordinarily different those two men were.

Even today, if one were to collect all the people I've ever encountered (both in physical and literary form), it would not be possible to find two individuals whose perspectives on life differed more than those of Abe Miner and Jim Newton (Grampy). In nearly every measure of what it means to be human, these men pushed the envelope in opposite directions.

Abe Miner, circa 1965.

Abe was the kind of man who would have felt at home in Ancient Greece, where pride was a virtue and individualism the ideal. Indeed, he would have immediately understood Achilles' choice, when that hero of *The Iliad* chose immortal fame (via a glorious death) over a safe but unsung homecoming.

Grampy, on the other hand, would have immediately tried to get Achilles the professional help he so desperately needed. How, Grampy would have wondered, could anyone choose fame over life? In Grampy's world, tales of heroic adventuring might make interesting reading, but what mattered most was spending time with family and friends.

*   *   *   *

Perhaps the best insight to Abe's story is to recognize just how much his life looked like a story—complete with adventure, obstacles, and most especially, conflict.

As anyone with even a passing knowledge of literature can attest, good storytelling requires conflict. From the classic *Hero's Journey* to the standard Hollywood movie of *Boy meets Girl*, the leading character's life is always in conflict and, therefore, always interesting.

Abe's life was always interesting.

In his world the only measure of success was accomplishment, and, if the Universe didn't provide the necessary ingredients, Abe would produce them himself.

It was not a path for the faint of heart or the contented. Instead, it was the path of a man who couldn't follow, couldn't relax, and couldn't abide the status quo.

Without doubt there is much to admire in a life such as Abe's and much justification in the pride and satisfaction he clearly felt for his many achievements, but it does make one wonder: Where does the "happily ever after" part fit in?

Now, I'm not suggesting that Abe's life was devoid of happiness. He clearly found winning against great odds magnificently satisfying, and Abe won against great odds every time he succeeded in business. But "happily ever after" implies a level of contentment and serenity that Abe never found particularly appealing. In other words (and to continue our story analogy), once the damsel's been saved and the quest fulfilled, there's nothing left that's interesting.

For Abe, a tale about a contented hero who takes long walks on the beach to watch beautiful sunsets wasn't a story worth living; it was a recipe for insignificance and boredom.

But what about the alternative: What if there was a contented hero? What if, rather than a life of doing, our contented hero found a life of service more satisfying? What if the happiness of others brought him more satisfaction than the accolades of personal achievement? Well, your name might be Grampy.

For the record, I'm not claiming sainthood for my maternal grandfather—Grampy had his faults. Moreover, he wasn't much above average by any of society's popular measurements. He wasn't rich; he wasn't brilliant; he wasn't musically talented, or beautiful, or famous. He wasn't any of the things modern culture holds dear. Yet, despite a life that was unexceptional in almost every way, Grampy remains the happiest man I've ever known.

By itself, this is more than noteworthy, but it becomes completely astonishing when one considers his background. Grampy's childhood alone should have crushed him. The oldest of four Irish emigrant children, he watched helplessly as his mother died from scarlet fever when he was 14. A few months later his father committed suicide. As a 15-year-old orphan, he saw his siblings sent away to live with relatives, while he was left to fend for himself.

Mere survival under those circumstances would have been remarkable, and surviving without becoming forever embittered nearly impossible, but that's just what Grampy did. Perhaps he had a kindly uncle. Perhaps there was a warm-hearted neighbor who helped him when he needed help most. I'd like to think so, but whatever happened, however he endured, the nearly miraculous outcome from this period of his life was that he maintained an assumption in the goodness of his fellow man and an abiding faith in God.

Particularly among my grandparents, Grampy's faith was unique. While Bee remained politely agnostic, Abe and Grammie (Peggie Newton) both thought all religion was rubbish, and that anyone who believed in a loving God—ready to intercede on their behalf—was ignoring a rather large and compelling body of evidence to the contrary.

Grampy believed otherwise. In his mind, the scientific view of the universe—one populated by atoms and ruled by physical laws—was far too simplistic. Instead, he looked at the heavens and saw a universe filled with beauty, infused with power, and magnificently ordered. It was a mechanism far greater than the sum of its parts, and one whose very existence cried out for a Creator.

From those premises, it was a short leap of faith to a benevolent God and the satisfying beliefs and rituals of Catholicism. For Grampy it was a relationship that quite literally satisfied his soul. Here he found the spiritual answers that had fulfilled humanity for two millennia: the reassurance of an afterlife, and the satisfaction that, in the end, justice prevailed.

Here was a faith that mirrored Grampy's innate sense of how the universe was supposed to work.

But enough of theology. The purpose here is not to judge or promote the merits of either Abe's or Grampy's conflicting religious feelings, but rather to show how those beliefs (or lack of belief) both reflected and reinforced each of their differing worldviews.

In Abe's world each individual was *independent*—responsible for his own destiny and always competing for his piece of the pie. Life was a challenge; a confrontation; a game where risk was required and winning mattered.

Grampy could scarcely imagine a life so isolated. He saw a world in which individuals were *interdependent*—where people both relied upon and helped one another. In his view, only people mattered. Everything else—work, investments, possessions—were a means to that end. Life was about planning the next backyard BBQ, or family outing, or Rotary Club function, or grandchild visit. It was about shared experiences with the people he loved.

⋆　　⋆　　⋆　　⋆

Kitty, Grampy, Steve (who must have been dressed by his sister for this picture) and the author, 1959.

Hard/soft; introverted/extroverted; solitary/social; thinker/feeler; Abe and Grampy were the Yin and Yang of the human experience, and their lives offer clear roadmaps down very different paths.

Each path offers compelling reasons to follow ...

CHAPTER 36

Miner's Hardware
(My Early Years)

As described elsewhere (through various timelines) Miner's Hardware in Grover Beach opened in 1956, when Lee and Glenn purchased a little hardware store on Grand Avenue.

According to my Dad's later stories, the first few months after opening were the stuff of retail nightmares—days when only a handful of customers walked through the doors. Nevertheless, they survived, and the business grew steadily. By the mid-1960s they had achieved two impressive milestones: the loan from their parents had been repaid; and they had moved into a new and much larger facility they had built next door (the hardware store's current location).

It wasn't quite a "rags-to-riches" story, but it was close, and both brothers were justifiably proud of their accomplishment. Unfortunately, their partnership had run its course and in 1966—in an amiable agreement—Lee and Glenn went their separate ways. Glenn held on to the hardware store and Lee went into the home appliance business.

Both brothers remained successful in their respective businesses, but by the mid-1970s and for a multitude of reasons Glenn's interest in the hardware store was in rapid decline. Ironically—and unknown to either party—as Glenn was agonizing over where his life had led, just across town at Miner's Home Appliance, I was losing interest in the appliance business and beginning to agonize over what new direction my life should take.

For more than a year Glenn quietly explored selling the hardware store, while just as quietly I was exploring opportunities elsewhere, when, in late 1978, an event which had always been considered impossible, happened: sales at Miner's Home Appliance began to exceed sales at Miner's Hardware.

Suddenly, Glenn saw a solution to his problem. A few weeks later, after receiving permission from my Dad, (a classy move on both their parts and a particularly gracious gesture from my Dad) Glenn made me an offer to become a partner in Miner's Hardware and take over its management. After much discussion between the three of us and an extended transition period between the two businesses, at age 27, I began my new career.

At the time, Miner's Hardware in Grover Beach was a small single-store operation. The building was about one-third its current size and there were only eight employees (four of whom were part-time). Still, it was a hell of an opportunity and a good fit for me on several levels. On the technical side I already knew the merchandise—I'd worked at the hardware store back in high school, and that, combined with my construction experience, meant that I knew how to use nearly everything we sold. On the management side of the business, Glenn was still using the same practices and procedures Abe had used a generation earlier back in Culver City. So, with a fresh eye, new ideas, and some long hours, I was soon making a big difference.

* * * *

Today, with nine busy locations and almost 400 employees, it's tempting to look back and imagine that Miner's Hardware's success followed a smooth upward trend that was all but pre-ordained.

I can assure the gentle reader that nothing could be further from the truth. When I arrived in 1979, we had competitors in every direction (most of whom were bigger and better than us); I knew considerably less about running a hardware store than I imagined; and Glenn had all but checked out of the business. In fact, after spending just a few days with me, he quickly settled into a routine that would last throughout most of our partnership: he'd show up late in the morning; we'd talk shop for about 10 minutes; then he'd disappear for the rest of the day.[43]

Surprisingly, it was an arrangement that suited us both—I wasn't particularly good at following directions and Glenn was only barely interested in the business. Fortunately for everyone, most of the decisions I made and the new things I tried worked. Just as importantly, whenever I did screwup (and this was not altogether infrequent) I was

---

43 Having already described much of our family's history with alcoholism, I want to deliberately skim over Glenn's. The condensed version is that at the beginning of our partnership he was typically intoxicated by mid-afternoon, which, because we rarely saw each other except in the morning, worked more or less. Over the years he tried quitting on several occasions and was once sober for almost a year, but he couldn't make it work. By his late 50s Glenn's alcoholism had worsened considerably, and for the last 15-plus years of his life, he was drunk most of the time.

usually quick to recognize my mistake and, because I *hated* screwing up, equally quick in figuring out how not to do it again.

By the mid-1980s the Grover store had been expanded twice, sales had risen substantially, and I was ready to open store #2. Glenn, not so much.

To be fair, while I was ready to risk everything I owned on the success of store #2, "everything" for me at that time wasn't a particularly large number. Glenn, on the other hand, stood to lose a considerable portion of his net worth, which he'd spent 30+ years building.

Incredibly, I managed to convince him to move forward, but it was a close thing—he nearly died from two directions.

First, in the months leading up to our Grand Opening, Miner's Hardware was spending money at a rate several times faster than anything Glenn had ever experienced, and the poor guy was experiencing nearly constant anxiety attacks.

Second, while I was up to my eyeballs with the countless details of opening a brand-new store, every few days Glenn would burst into my office and breathlessly announce that we had to walk away from our expansion plans. Each time I'd have to stop what I was doing and spend the next 20 minutes or so trying to talk him down from the ceiling. He'd eventually calm down, agree that we should proceed, and then in two or three days we'd do it all over again. It was exhausting, and after the first dozen or so incidents I was ready to put him out of his misery with my bare hands.

Fortunately, for my sanity and Glenn's continued earthly existence, the Arroyo Grande Store opened on time in the Fall of 1986 and was immediately profitable—an outcome far more illuminating than one might guess …

When I first proposed opening the Arroyo Grande Store only two miles from our Grover Beach Store, most everyone thought I was an idiot. When it succeeded, I suddenly became a genius. Neither group was entirely wrong.

While I never doubted that the Arroyo Store would succeed, I was blissfully unaware of one extremely relevant statistic: on average, a new hardware store isn't profitable until year three. (Fortunately, Miner's Hardware has always beaten that average, but even with our enviable track record only two of our next seven stores turned a profit in the first month.) So, when the Arroyo store opened, I had no plan and no money to support an unprofitable location. Our immediate success, therefore, was absolutely crucial and a lasting testament to that old cliché: "it's better to be lucky than smart."

But, before we continue with the saga of Miner's Hardware, we need to catch up on world events, discover what our remaining characters are up to, and introduce two new characters who will play critical roles as our story progresses.

CHAPTER 37

Moving at Hyperspeed

The 1980s are sometimes referred to as the "Decade of Greed" or the "Decade of Decadence" which, frankly, seems a real disservice to all the decades that have followed. I mean really, when was the last time you heard anyone say, "Gee, there sure seems to be a lot less greed and decadence today than in decades past?"

Instead, it's always seemed to me that the more accurate (and catchier) title for the 1980s should have been *The Age of Acronyms.*

During that decade the IBM PC, CD's, and VHS all made their debut—each a never-before-seen wonder that created entirely new industries. The movie *E.T.* became the highest grossing film of the decade, while GMOs, IVF, and (tragically) AIDS all made their first appearances.[44] It was also the decade that first introduced WWW (World Wide Web) a technology so revolutionarily disruptive that

---

44 Acronym decoder: IBM Personal Computer, Compact Disk, Video Home System, Extra Terrestrial, Genetically Modified Organism, In-vitro Fertilization (test tube baby) Acquired Immune Deficiency Syndrome.

even now—nearly 40 years later—neither government, industry, nor society understand where it's going or how to control it.

Yet, despite the lasting fame and significance of the above-mentioned examples, my "age of acronyms" idea never got any traction, and today the 1980s are increasingly associated with *The Information Age*—arguably the most consequential period in human history.

It turns out that, until somewhere around 1850, human knowledge was doubling about every century. That began to change dramatically with the Industrial Revolution (e.g., mass production of steel in 1870, first skyscraper 1885, first airplane 1903) and then really changed in 1951, when the first commercial computer became operational. After that it was like growth on steroids, and before the end of the 1980s it was estimated that human knowledge was doubling every year!

This was change at a level humanity had never imagined let alone experienced, which, coincidently, is exactly what I was experiencing on a personal level. Indeed, of all the decades I've lived through (which is now getting uncomfortably close to double digits) the 1980s remain at the top of my *Repeat List*.

To be clear, I'm not talking about a do-over because of regrets, but rather a chance to appreciate all that was happening, because I swear my world throughout the 1980s was moving at hyper-speed.

Honestly, as I look back at this period from my current 72-year-old perspective, it seems impossible. Besides all that was happening at Miner's Hardware (which was not inconsequential), I partially followed in my father's footsteps by getting my General Contractor's and private pilot's licenses. Separately from the business and with borrowed money, I built a few single-family homes and started a small handful of real estate partnerships. In my spare time (among other interests), I was jumping off mountain tops in a hang glider, diligently reading my way through the 100 Greatest Books, and running at least 20 miles per week—competing regularly in 10Ks, a few longer races, and one marathon.

How resplendent it would be to feel that kind of energy again (for a little while anyway).

Yet, by far the best and most important experiences from this period were that Susie and I had become parents, and what could be better than spending more time with our daughters, Amy and Bethany, when they were little girls?

We had countless adventures together. Most were as simple as "forts" in the living room or safaris in the sand dunes, a few as almighty as Disneyland or climbing Half Dome in Yosemite, and I'd give nearly anything to do them all again.

Altogether, it was a decade full of extraordinary times: first steps, first day of school, first backpack trip—all those first-in-a-lifetime events which were awesome for the girls and usually more so for their parents. But, beyond our little foursome there was someone else who was constantly making our lives better, and it is to that remarkable woman's story that we return to next.

CHAPTER 38

The Buddha Nature of Bee

For Bee and Grammie, the deaths of their husbands brought an abrupt and unwelcome end to nearly 50 years of marriage, companionship, and routine. Intellectually, they both understood the situation. In fact, from about middle age onward, they had both suspected this day would come, but no amount of rational thought could anticipate the emotional force of losing a lifelong partner.

For Grammie it was catastrophic. Trapped between anger and despair over Grampy's death, her life began a slow downward spiral into bitterness and victimhood—a combination so unpleasant that, eventually, old friends deserted her while family remained only to the extent duty required.

Her world got smaller every year.

Bee, as in most everything, followed a different path. Certainly, she felt the loss of her husband. In fact, some 15 years after Abe's death, Bee once made the haunting observation that, "Days or even weeks can pass without me thinking about Abe, but then I'll slip and in the middle of a book, or a TV program, turn to say something and realize the room is empty."

It must have been brutal. Forty-eight years of living beside Abe at work and at home and then, over just a few months, a forced transition to being alone. But, as with every other adversity the Universe had thrown her way, Bee rolled with it because at the core of her being she believed something Grammie never could: *Everything Works Out for the Best.*

Even as a child I can remember Bee trying to comfort me with that message, although, frankly, I had almost as much trouble swallowing it as Grammie did. Worse, the older I got, the harder it was to square Bee's philosophy against all of life's misfortunes, and it seemed absolutely impossible when juxtaposed against her own experience.

I mean, seriously, as far as I could tell, Bee's life hadn't just been visited by adversity; it had been attacked. Like something out of the *Book of Job*, she had suffered through much: the early death of her father, the cruel loss of two infant sons, the alcoholism of her husband and both surviving sons, financial ruin on two occasions, the afflictions of arthritis and palsy, and, finally, the deaths of her husband, her oldest son, all her siblings, and every single one of her contemporaries.

Surely, I reasoned, Bee's unshakable conviction that *Everything Works Out for the Best* was rubbish—the same silly mistake Voltaire had so famously satirized in *Candide*: a mindless denial of all life's tragedies.

However, it never really mattered to Bee what I (or anyone else) thought. Despite all the suffering she experienced herself and all the injustice she saw around her, she remained steadfast. To every setback and misfortune life delivered, Bee's consoling words and heartfelt belief remained constant: *Everything Works Out for the Best.*

In the beginning it was easy for me to dismiss her philosophy as being overly simplistic or even delusional; however, as the years went by, I couldn't help but notice a curious and recurring problem with my dismissal, because against all odds and all common sense, Bee's life almost always *did* work out for the best.

It didn't make sense. Somehow, in Bee's world, cause and effect had become disentangled, stimulus and response unaligned. What was going on?

The secret, I finally realized, was that Bee was cheating. She was actually making *Everything Work Out for the Best*—a trick so difficult and unusual that I've only ever seen it performed by a small handful of people who were either deeply religious or had spent years studying and practicing some form of spirituality.

However, in a pattern similar to just about every other aspect of her life, Bee didn't fit those molds either. She never studied philosophy and very deliberately rejected all forms of religion and theology. Instead, blessed with extraordinary insight and intuition, she seems to have independently discovered and embraced a long list of shared truths that lie at the heart of most spiritual traditions—especially Stoicism and Buddhism.

It's embarrassing, really; I grew up with one of the greatest teachers on the planet and it was decades before I began to recognize how wise she really was. Frankly, I might never have figured it out at all if it hadn't been for a pair of Zen masters who (in just four paragraphs) will join us for breakfast …

CHAPTER 39

Breakfast at Bee's

After Abe died, Bee and I were both reluctant to end our regular visits, and we soon settled into a new routine. Every Monday, Wednesday, and Friday I'd arrive at her house about 7 a.m. to be greeted by a table that was already set and the smell of just-cooked bacon. This was generally accompanied by scrambled eggs, although pancakes, hash browns, and avocado toast were frequent substitutions. In addition, there was orange juice and coffee on the table, and, just above my napkin and silverware, a treat. This was for me to eat later when I got hungry at work.

I loved my treat. It might be a candy bar, or some cookies, or a peanut butter and jelly sandwich, but it was always waiting for me, and it always made me smile.

I smiled partially because of the unspoken game it represented: unable to convince Bee that I was too old for a treat, I dutifully took it with me to work each morning (to be placed in the employee break room next to the donut box). But mostly, I smiled because throughout my childhood Bee had always been my biggest fan, and each time I held my treat, it reminded me she still was.

Altogether I shared thousands of breakfasts with Bee—from infancy right up through middle age—and, while most of them have blurred together, there remain a few score and more that I remember with clarity. Some of those memories connect to the typical events that fill a life—births, deaths, successes, failures, and so on. More than a few are from moments when Bee said something so profound or so insightful that it felt like I was being whacked with some kind of metaphysical two-by-four, but of all the time we spent together, the memories I treasure the most are when my daughters, Amy and Bethany, joined me at Grammie Bee's kitchen table.[45]

As soon as Amy could eat solid food, I began taking her with me on my breakfast adventures (in late 1979). Bethany followed about 18 months later (the difference in their ages), and throughout their childhood it was a rare Wednesday morning that didn't find the three of us sharing breakfast together with Grammie Bee. In time, with the dual pressures of adolescence and academics, the girls' visits became less regular, but even into college they would still accompany me on occasion or, more often, visit on their own as their schedules allowed.

Our visits to Grammie Bee's kitchen would last almost 20 years—a period in which those little girls grew into womanhood as they and their great-grandmother continued to reach across four generations and find delight in each other's company. It was a period filled with

---

45 I only ever knew my paternal grandparents by their first names, Abe and Bee. So did everyone else including their sons, friends, and the rest of their grandchildren. Susie, however, always found this level of familiarity appalling and insisted our daughters call their great-grandmother "Grammie Bee."

stories (some of which we'll get to in later chapters), and one of the best happened early on …

Around the time Bethany turned 4 years old, she discovered that eggs could be cooked in ways other than scrambled. It wasn't that she actually cared about the difference in taste or texture, but for a very little girl "sunny-side up" and "over-easy" were wonderfully exciting options. So, on our very next visit to her great-grandmother's house, Bethany immediately ran into the kitchen to ask Grammie Bee if she could have her egg over-easy.

Having lived with shaking hands for decades and caught momentarily off-guard, Bee automatically replied, "No."

Then, after a second's thought, and to Bethany's startled expression (it was the first time Bethany had ever heard Grammie Bee say, "No") Bee reached down, gave Bethany a quick hug and offered, "Well, I can try…but it's probably going to come out scrambled anyway."

The result, I'm afraid, was an egg that looked more like it had been *assaulted* by the spatula Bee was holding rather than gently flipped. Indeed, it didn't look like any kind of egg I'd ever seen before, and I immediately worried that Bee would be both embarrassed and frustrated by her inability to succeed at such a simple task.

It was a waste of worry. Bee was as undisturbed as Bethany was thrilled. In the innocence and excitement of childhood Bethany saw an egg that was different from scrambled as something special and wonderful—something made just for her. Bee, with the wisdom and experience of almost 80 years, knew what was important and what wasn't. Her great-granddaughter was important. Hugs were important, but an egg was just an egg.

It was such a little exchange—over in the blink of an eye and never repeated—yet so quintessentially Bee. By a hundred little examples of kindness and listening, by a hundred more of humility and love, Bee took us to school at every visit and we never knew it.

… except for a single test near the end.

CHAPTER 40

Miner's Hardware in the '90s

Every decade seems extraordinary to the people who are living through it, but even allowing for this built-in bias the 1990s were special. With the collapse of the USSR (in 1991) and China's rise from a third-world country still in its infancy, the "Nineties" marked the zenith of America's power. Economically, militarily, and technologically our Country reigned supreme among the nations of the Earth.

Domestically, conditions were just as exceptional—a decade of peace and prosperity, when the stock market tripled in value, real wages increased, and the U.S. Congress agreed to a balanced budget.[46]

In fact, so many events were moving in a positive direction that one could easily imagine those long-ago editors at the *New York Times* (see page 2) pointing to the 1990s as the manifestation of "the brighter

---

46 Few examples better illustrate the exceptionalness of the 1990s than the national debt. From 1950 onward, the federal government consistently ran a deficient; however, by the late 1990s this had reversed, and the country entered the new millennium (2000) with a budget surplus of $236 billion dollars. It's been in free fall ever since. Today (2024), it stands at minus $3.5 trillion dollars —15 times greater, but in the wrong direction!

dawn" they had so confidently predicted at the beginning of the 20th century.

Yet, as clairvoyant as their prediction had proven to be, there was something fundamentally different about the 1990s that no one at the turn of the century had foreseen: change wasn't just happening faster than ever before; it was accelerating. We were living in *Exponential Times.*[47]

On the surface this sounds harmless enough, but change is always disruptive and for Miner's Hardware the explosion of Big Box stores looked to be cataclysmic. All across the country, small local drug stores, bookstores, departments stores, and more—family businesses that had survived for generations—closed their doors. Hardware stores in particular went out of business by the thousands, and everybody that was left wondered if they'd be next.

Should that last paragraph sound melodramatic, consider what this looked like in real-time: by 1999 Miner's Hardware had four locations, each about 15,000 sq. ft. in size.[48] A typical Home Depot was over 100,000 sq. ft. (a few were twice that size). This meant that our entire "empire" of four stores would have easily fit inside *one* of their locations ... with more than an acre of building left over. More worrisome still, Home Depot was growing like a virus: from just over

---

47   It's very likely that somewhere in elementary school your math teacher assigned some version of the following problem: "If you start with a penny and double the amount every day, how much will you have by the end of one month?" At the end of the first week, you only have 64 cents (1, 2, 4, 8, 16, 32, 64). By the end of the second week, you're still less than a hundred bucks at $81.92, but then "magic" starts to happen and by the end of the month you're a multi-millionaire with $10,737,418.24! That's exponential growth.

48   These stores were later expanded and today each of our locations are about 20,000 sq. ft.

100 stores in 1990, they were adding a new Home Depot every other *day* by the end of the decade and soon passed 2,000 locations.

In the meantime, Amazon had opened for business in 1994 and internet sales were quickly becoming the new retail disrupter—taking out family businesses and big box stores alike. (Anyone remember Linens 'n Things, Borders Bookstore, or Circuit City?)

However, as unnerving as all this was, disruption usually cuts both ways. So, as marginal hardware stores went out of business, Miner's Hardware found itself in the right place at the right time to expand.

Still, it was a scary process. As always, risk and reward remained intertwined, but the difference in the 1990s was that almost everything I thought I knew about business was changing and then changing again, which meant that each expansion became a journey into the unknown.

Yet, as anxiety producing as the '90s were to Miner's Hardware, it was nothing compared to the rest of my world where all the change driven by living in Exponential Times managed to sync itself with the change only experienced by fathers whose daughters turn into teenagers, progress through high school, enter college, and then go off to live their own lives.

This was CHANGE in capital letters and every piece of it seemed to arrive trailing two conditions: it was always uncomfortable; and it usually came with a lesson.

Why this happens remains a mystery. Maybe the Universe simply enjoys making people uncomfortable, or maybe some people can only learn lessons the hard way. Regardless, I can tell you that throughout my 40s (which nearly matched the decade of the 1990s) lessons were being presented from every direction and with such unnerving frequency that I soon recognized myself in an old piece of wisdom which declares:

Every day the Universe will present you with lessons.

You may not like the lesson, but it will be repeated until you learn it.

You will then be free to move onto the next lesson.

The next chapter provides a glimpse into some of those uncomfortable lessons ...

CHAPTER 41

Three Lessons from the '90s

Madden's Lesson

Full confession, I'm not much of a sports guy. True, I enjoy playing sports (and was once fairly adept at basketball) but I've never found the spectator side of the equation all that interesting. So, when anybody talks about the "Big Game" or player stats, or first round draft picks, my mind is a blank, which is why I had no idea how impressed I should have been when I was introduced to one of sport's best-known personalities.

It was the mid-1990s when, along with a small handful of fellow hardware store owners, I was in the LA area to attend a regional meeting with Ace's Management Team.[49] It was a typical meeting—meaning that I've long since forgotten everything on the agenda—except that after the lunch break one of the staff members excitedly announced that we were about have a surprise visit from Ace's new spokesperson, John Madden.

---

49 Ace Hardware is a buying co-op owned by nearly 5,000 individual Ace Dealers. Miner's Hardware is one of those owners.

There was a collective gasp from the audience and in walks this huge guy with no neck, a size 4-X chest, and a disarming smile. Apparently, he was somebody important because the half-dozen guys fidgeting around me all seemed unsure whether they should bow or genuflect.

Still clueless, I watched our surprise guest move to the front of the room and with unassuming ease begin telling stories one after the other. He was a gifted speaker and one of the most charismatic humans I've ever met, but my real takeaway from this chance encounter was Madden's story about coaching the Oakland Raiders (which I correctly surmised was a football team).

Hired as the youngest coach in NFL history, Madden would go on to have a win-record that has yet to be equaled, because, he explained, he knew something about people that few understood.

"There are three kinds of people," he pronounced.

- Those who *don't* know what's happening.

- Those who *do* know what's happening

- Those who *make* things happen.

"Most organizations," he continued, "spend their energy trying to weed out the first kind and attract the second kind. I was only interested in the third kind."

Almost instantly I recognized my mistake.

Our third store in Morro Bay had recently opened, and it wasn't going well. Sales were below expectations and my first two picks for the store manager position had been just short of disastrous—they had both been technically competent (i.e., they knew what was happening) but they couldn't *make* things happen.

Once Madden had pointed out the obvious, I knew what to look for and was soon able to find the right person for the job.

It was an "Aha" moment of the first order—one that had an immediate and lasting effect on the success of Miner's Hardware. However, while the family business would continue to dispense lessons with unasked for frequency, most of the truly "Aha" moments came from elsewhere, and two of the most memorable arrived via the women I lived with.

The Girls' Lesson

As the 1990s advanced, so too did Amy and Bethany. Which, especially during their teenage years, resulted in (more than a few) episodes of discomfort and anxiety for their father. Gratefully, Grammie Bee's advice and reassurance during those "turbulent teens" saved my parental life on multiple occasions. Yet, as helpful as her wisdom and experience often were, there was something else going on at her house that I didn't fully appreciate until much later.

Meeting at Grammie Bee's kitchen table was like entering Switzerland—a place everyone recognized as neutral territory. Here the father-daughter dynamic was suspended. Instead, in the presence of Grammie Bee, we were grandchildren and great-grandchildren, and that shift changed everything. Conversations, ideas, suggestions, and questions that were difficult or even impossible elsewhere were usually open for consideration. Sometimes with surprising effect ...

From the time they were toddlers, the girls loved hearing Grammie Bee's stories about growing up on a farm in the early 1900s. They knew, for example, that when their great-grandmother was a little girl, milk came fresh and warm from the family cow that lived in the barn. Because there was no electricity, they knew that turning on the lights meant lighting a kerosene lamp and that water came from a hand pump in the front yard. They knew that the family's single bathroom was an outhouse.

For the girls, however, all this information was abstract. They could imagine the lack of all modern conveniences—no electricity, no bathroom, and no running water. In fact, they had experienced those very conditions on numerous backpack trips we'd taken together, but it wasn't part of their everyday life. It wasn't real. For the girls, computers were real, pagers (those precursors to cell phones) were real, and, because they were in their early teens at this point in our story, boys were starting to become real.

Indeed, as any father of young teenage girls can tell you, the list of new realities is downright staggering. So, imagine, if you will, that on an otherwise nondescript morning in 1992, this particular father has just sat down to a quiet breakfast with his grandmother and her 13 and 14-year-old great-granddaughters, when he suddenly realizes the morning's conversation has turned to tampons.

Imagine further that the girls have just made the startling discovery that their great-grandmother had lived from puberty all the way through menopause *before* tampons had been invented.

Naturally, I took this as my cue to try blending into the wallpaper just as my three table mates began discussing the pros and cons of various feminine hygiene products the way guys might talk about different brands of sports equipment.

Completely at ease, Bee was clearly warming to the subject at hand and had an expression that looked as if she was searching for an old book—one that had been laid on a high shelf and not opened for ages. It took a moment, but she soon produced a memory that had been tucked away for more than 70 years. It was a story Bee appeared never to have told before and, yet, as it unfolded, a story that seemed to be as fresh and clear in her mind as the day it happened.

It must have been about 1918, she explained, when her first period began, and in the telling it was obvious even to me that Bee had been just as scared and mortified and proud as her great-granddaughters were four generations later. However, there existed a rather noteworthy difference between their respective experiences that had to do with a small box Bee's mother had given her.

It looked a bit like a small square purse, Bee told us, with a little handle on top, but instead of "purse stuff," it held a few of the dozen pads her mother had made by sewing cheesecloth around thick pieces of cotton.

It got worse, because, just as the girls and I were coming to terms with the task of producing all those pads every month, Bee casually mentioned they were designed to be washed by hand and reused.

I must say that the recycling aspect of this story caught Grammie Bee's entire audience completely by surprise, and I could see the girls turning the concept of reusable pads over in their minds, where it immediately got stuck in a loop between disbelief and dread. Grammie Bee's small box was bad enough, the handmade pads worse, but this new disclosure was producing an almost apoplectic response from her great-granddaughters.

Yet, even as the girls were repelled and appalled, they couldn't wait to ask more questions.

As the conversation continued (without me, of course), I realized for the first time that my teenage daughters were engaged in a conversation between *women*. Moreover, and to their increasing delight, the girls not only found themselves on equal footing with their great-grandmother, they had something they could teach her.

For a moment it felt like I had stumbled into a girls' locker room, or slumber party, or baby shower, or some other female bonding ritual, because, I swear, estrogen was starting to condense right out of the air.

Unlike boys, girls get absolutely clobbered by puberty, and the significance of that single event is something all women share. All by itself (and this is on top of breasts and births and God-knows-what-else), puberty connects women in a way so fundamental that it spans time and culture, and all this was being played out right in front of me across four generations.

Don't misunderstand. I quite like being a boy, and I see little to recommend 30-plus years of monthly cramps, tampons, and mood swings. Still, I couldn't help but wonder if it might not be worth it, because on that morning, as I continued watching my daughters and grandmother interact, it occurred to me that being male meant I would forever be denied an astonishing portion of the human experience.

Susie's Lesson

As previously revealed (see Chapter 32), I dropped out of college when I was 19. It was the right decision at the time, but one I would eventually regret. Twenty-three years later, at age 42, I returned.

It was an unusual arrangement that required two full years of (primarily) independent study combined with a weekly 160-mile roundtrip drive to Santa Barbara, but it worked well for me.

Partially, it worked because I was a more mature and motivated student, but mostly it worked because the university I chose for my second attempt mostly allowed me to pick the classes I wanted to take.[50] But even with all their flexibility, the university still required a few courses I couldn't avoid, and one of those was clinical psychology.

It was a class filled with students half my age and every one of them aspired to become a practicing therapist. As a group they were kind, well-meaning, and, so far as I could tell, completely incapable of analytical thought. Instead, like beings from another planet, they all emoted their way through life.

Surprisingly, it was the bit about planets that would prove to be important.

The class focused on various methods of psychotherapy, each of which had a different focus: mind, behavior, childhood, music, and so on. The idea was that different individuals will respond more or less well to different avenues of therapy.

---

50 I'd managed to talk my way into Cal Poly's Executive MBA program (without an undergraduate degree), but after reviewing the MBA curriculum with two different professors, I quickly decided against that path. Instead, I opted for Antioch University—an old liberal arts school with a satellite campus in Santa Barbara.

To my left-brain, business-oriented intellect, they all sounded like nothing more than a marketing strategy—and a poorly conceived strategy at that. So, imagine my state of mind—it's late one evening at home and I'm sitting at my desk trying to write a paper for this "stupid class"—when my wife, Susie, happens to walk by...

Me: ... Listen to this drivel. "Using the Hakomi Method, the therapist's role is to provide a loving presence."

Susie: And ...?

Me: Look, if I'm going to take the trouble of hiring an expert like a CPA, or an attorney, or a therapist, I don't want to pay some knucklehead to be a loving presence. I want *answers*.

Susie: (slight pause) You sound just like a Martian.

Me: (a longer and completely confused pause) A Martian? What the hell does that mean?

Susie: I just finished reading, *Men are from Mars; Women are from Venus*, and, according to the author, most men (Martians) immediately go into fix-it mode when confronted with a problem, while most women (Venusians) first want to discuss their feelings about the problem.

Me: ... So, are you saying that men want to fix the problem and women just want to bitch about it?

Susie: NO. (long pause—which we both knew contained an unspoken expletive regarding my person) When I have a problem, I want you to acknowledge my feelings. When you, instead, immediately tell me how I should have fixed the problem, it feels like you're telling me I made a mistake.

I should mention here that no single conversation has ever made less sense to me. What possible benefit, I wondered, could wallowing in one's emotions bring to problem solving? It was such a bizarre concept that the very next week I read the book Susie had referenced. It didn't help. Despite the fact that the author presented some good arguments and backed them up with examples even I could follow, I still wasn't buying it.

It was at this point that the Universe interceded with one of its "Mother-of-all-Lessons."

Only days after reading Susie's Men-are-from-Mars book, I happened to arrive at a luncheon exactly as late as an old friend did. Because of our mutual tardiness, the two of us were seated at a table by ourselves, and it was here that I began to all but gush about my immediate crisis: earlier that morning a business deal I had been working on for more than a year had suddenly blown up, and the repercussions were going to be seriously consequential.

My friend listened politely and after thinking carefully for a moment offered three possible solutions in quick succession.

I'd already considered the first two and the last "solution" was unworkable, but within my friend's suggestions what I heard most clearly was a piece of my brain shouting, "Holy Shit! This guy is trying to *fix* me" even as the rest of me was pleading for more time. I wasn't ready to be fixed; instead, I first needed to spend some time sorting out my feelings.

It was an "Aha" moment so powerful, so uncomfortable, and so very "Venusian" that for a good long while afterwards I wondered if I should be taking testosterone supplements.

*   *   *   *

Altogether, navigating the 1990s was a challenge unlike anything I'd ever experienced, which (I hope) helps explain why I was talking to my long-deceased grandfathers.

Knowing those men as well as I did and recognizing the extreme differences in how they perceived and engaged with the world, meant that I could all but hear the conflicting counsel my grandfathers might offer.

So, whenever I found myself confronted with important or difficult decisions (like how to simultaneously survive teenage daughters and Home Depot), deliberating the pros and cons of a particular choice with my grandfathers would often bring much needed clarity to my internal decision-making process.

It still does ... but not always.

Especially as I got older and life's challenges became more complex, I found myself in want of a third opinion—someone to help me triangulate my position, to cast a deciding vote.

Incredibly, the Universe obliged. It just took me a while to figure it out, because this guy, rather than being a role model to follow, only led by counterexample. [51]

---

51 Editor's Note: Apparently, the Universe so thoroughly enjoyed providing me with lessons throughout my 40s that, shortly after reaching my 50s (and without my knowledge or consent), it enrolled me in a 29-day advanced course, which is chronicled in my (only) other book: *Following John Muir: Searching for Enlightenment at 10,000'*

CHAPTER 42

Glenn

By the early 1990s (about the time Glenn turned 60) my relationship with my uncle began to seriously decline …then it got worse. This was most unfortunate because—and I'm speaking with real authority here—about the only thing worse than having a difficult partner is having one for a really long time.

Glenn and I would be partners for nearly 30 years.

By itself the fact that Glenn became difficult is hardly noteworthy—everybody has to deal with difficult people. In fact, difficult people are so commonplace it's tempting to believe they're some kind of requirement. Perhaps, they're necessary for cosmic balance, or maybe they're here just to keep things interesting, But, whatever their purpose, the Universe—which was already throwing lessons at me with enthusiasm—now appeared intent on having Glenn take me to school in a completely new format. And as I look back, the first thing I learned from my uncle was about learning itself …

By his own admission, Glenn never read a book in his life. Not even a chapter. Nor did he read magazines or newspapers. And it wasn't just reading he disliked. He never watched the news on television or listened to it on the radio. He never took a class or attended a seminar.

Now, I realize some people just aren't all that curious, but Glenn's self-imposed ignorance was extraordinary. Unburdened by facts, he believed whatever his feelings dictated—a method that rarely produced good outcomes. Even in business, as Miner's Hardware grew and became more complicated, Glenn refused to adapt. True, he always knew where to find "net profit" on our financial statements, but almost every other number and how they tied together remained a mystery. Regarding computers, Glenn would never even learn how to turn one on, let alone how to use it.

With a record like his, one could easily be forgiven in assuming Glenn was mentally challenged, and over the years I frequently considered that possibility. But there was a singular and fatal problem with this theory that had to do with fishing.

Like his parents and brother, Glenn loved everything about fishing, and by the time my tribulations with him were becoming serious, he would often take his 24-foot fishing boat as much as 50 miles offshore to fish for albacore (about 40 miles beyond a visible shoreline).

Of course, one could argue this simply proves the point (i.e., only a fool would take such a small boat 50 miles out into the open ocean). The problem, however, was that this "fool" kept finding his way home. Without radar, without modern navigation equipment (this was long before GPS), Glenn had taught himself how to navigate with a magnetic compass and a primitive radio system called LORAN.

So, in a life-or-death situation (assuming it involved *his* life or death), Glenn was able to learn as well as the next guy. Nevertheless, he must have found the process thoroughly displeasing, because *only* the threat of certain death could motivate him to learn anything new.

Not surprisingly, Glenn's conspicuous lack of relevant information, combined with his worsening alcoholism, led to an ever-increasing number of poor choices, and by the mid-1990s his personal life was beginning to unfold like a Greek tragedy—the hero destroyed by a combination of personal failings and circumstances he cannot control.

Like everyone, he wanted to be happy, and by now Glenn had attained what he most desired: wealth and leisure. He had more money than he'd ever dreamed possible, and he'd long since stopped working. In quick succession he bought a new car, a new truck, and a new travel trailer. He bought a new boat and a new house. He even went to Mexico and bought a new vacation home in Baja California. Nothing worked.

A MINER SIDE NOTE

GLENN'S STUFF

Despite unmitigated failure, Glenn forever believed that more "stuff" was bound to make him happier. He had stuff everywhere—much of it never used and some in boxes that had never been opened. But of all his mindless consumption, the most absurd example must surely have been his sizable collection of books.

Never read (and touched only when the housekeeper dusted them), Glenn's library was chosen not by author or subject, but rather by size and color.

For a long while I assumed Glenn's behavior was the classic "Money-Can't-Buy-Happiness" lesson, but that was only part of the answer. The underlying cause proved to be much deeper and the first clue to figuring it out began with a hamburger …

Just as he was leaving my office after his typical morning visit (about 1995), Glenn mentioned that he was heading to McDonald's for their special.

"Special?" I asked.

"They're selling regular hamburgers four for a dollar," Glenn replied enthusiastically.

"Four hamburgers? How are you going to eat four hamburgers? It's not even noon yet!"

"I'm not," he explained. "I'm going to get five bucks' worth and freeze them for later."

"Later?" I asked in disbelief. "You're going to freeze a McDonald's hamburger, then thaw it out for lunch at some future date? And you want to do this 20 times?!"

"Yeah!" and away he went.

Now I've eaten my share of fast food (particularly in the 1980s and 1990s traveling constantly between the stores), and with all those years of experience I can confidently report that a regular McDonald's hamburger is quite literally at the bottom of the fast-food food chain. Even served fresh and hot off the griddle, they're nearly as tasteless as the wax paper they come wrapped in. So, the idea of eating one of those things after it's been frozen and then "nuked" in a microwave was all but unthinkable. Taking deliberate steps to have this experience 20 times was simply beyond imagination.

As Glenn hurried away for his appointment with cold, nasty food, I sat alone in my office slowly replaying our conversation and trying to make sense of it all. "Mike," I finally said (out loud, as I recall), "There's something seriously wrong with your partner."

On the one hand, Glenn was spending money like someone who'd just won the lottery. Yet, here he was freezing 25-cent hamburgers to save money! It didn't make sense. Of course, most of what Glenn did didn't make sense, and I assumed this was just another example of his increasingly irrational behavior.

I was mistaken. It turned out there actually was a pattern to the hamburger mystery, and not long afterwards Glenn provided the final clue, when he recounted a conversation with a young man who had recently asked him, "When is enough [money] enough?"

Amazingly, this most basic of questions had never before occurred to Glenn, but after some quick and serious thought he soon proclaimed, "There's never enough!"

Relating this story in my office, Glenn was so proud of his answer that he repeated the ending a second time with added emphasis on *never*, then, certain he'd just shared the most remarkable insight of the age, waited expectantly for my applause, or endorsement, or at least a nod of appreciation.

Suddenly, everything fell into place. Money had always played a disproportionate role in Glenn's life, but somewhere along the way it had become another addiction. The more he had, the more he wanted, and that insatiable craving was behind much of his worsening behavior.

No wonder he was eating reheated hamburgers. Every nickel he didn't have diminished him.

No wonder his handshake agreements had become worthless. If "there's never enough," then his old values of integrity and fairness were no longer of consequence.

No wonder he was always buying things. If money was the most important thing in one's life, then displays of wealth were the measure of one's success.

Tragically, Glenn would continue to provide me with lessons right up until his death in 2008. No matter the circumstance, no matter how many times he'd made the same mistake before, from about his mid-fifties onward the guy made bad choices at every opportunity. In fact, Glenn would demonstrate *How Not to Lead a Life* with such unnerving consistency that even today, whenever I'm faced with a tricky decision, my first thought is to imagine what Glenn would have done and eliminate that choice with prejudice.

In so many ways Glenn was like his father—both of them stubborn businessmen who loved making money and loved the outdoors. In his old age Glenn even began to look like Abe: the same height, the same pudgy frame, even the same small bald spot on the top of his head. More to the point, until their middle 50s, both men had been similarly crippled by alcoholism.

Yet, somehow, Abe had found the courage and determination to control his inner demons, where Glenn never could. In defeating alcoholism, Abe quite literally changed his life's trajectory. As he grew older, he found meaning and purpose in his personal life and a renewed sense of accomplishment in his professional life.

Unable to summon the personal resolve of his father, Glenn turned instead towards his addictions and all but embraced them. In the end—and in the cruelest of ironies—they both died exactly as they had lived.

CHAPTER 43

Other Voices

A few months after Glenn's funeral (May 2008), I happened to cross paths with one of his old contemporaries. The two of us spoke briefly, exchanged a few pleasantries, and soon he was relating how much he missed my uncle.

Yes, Glenn had some issues, the man acknowledged, but that didn't mean he wasn't a decent guy and a good friend.

It was an observation impossible to reconcile with my experience, but that brief conversation forced me to remember that how we see one another and the world in general is always a subjective experience.[52]

Which brings us directly to the messy task of this book: telling someone else's story. What facts to include, what to ignore, their order and emphasis—all bear on the story's outcome; yet all are controlled by the author.

---

52 Our experience is also in constant flux as people change, circumstances change, and we, as observers, change. All of us ebbing and flowing as the years fly by. (I am not the first person to figure this out.)

It seems only fair, therefore, that other voices should be heard, and to that end we begin with a spoiler alert: Grammie's life doesn't finish well. It doesn't play particularly well in the middle either. She had no professional career, wasn't very social, and lacked any marketable skills. In Grammie's version of the world, her life's purpose was that of a wife and mother, and when those roles disappeared, so too, did her life's meaning.

Yet, as accurate as that synopsis remains, I'm no longer confident it tells the truth.

This is entirely my sister's fault, because, immediately after reading an early draft of that last paragraph, Kitty demanded to know why I hadn't mentioned the years Grammie volunteered at a well-baby clinic for disadvantaged mothers. (I'd forgotten about that.) Then she added, "And your earlier assertion that Grammie never got dirty or went on adventures," she fumed, "is nonsense!"

Delivered in her "Mom" voice (an ability that I swear she's had since childhood), Kitty's message was clear: *her big brother didn't know what he was talking about.*

It was an attitude I've learned to be wary of, but before I could begin my defense, Kitty, who had been furiously thumbing through an old photo album, victoriously pointed to a picture of Grammie standing next to a waterfall.

Our grandmother looked to be in her late 40s, and on the back of the picture were the words "Nevada Falls, Yosemite." In disbelief I recognized the setting. I've been to Nevada Falls, and the only way one can arrive at that location is to traverse a trail of nasty switchbacks that ascend more than 2,000 vertical feet above the valley floor.

Even assuming she'd arrived on horseback (an option not available today), it was still an impossible achievement for a woman I could only remember being in the kitchen, but there was Grammie—standing near the edge of the falls in shoes with heels, wearing a dress, and smiling at her accomplishment.

Still staring at the picture and the epic inconsistency it represented, my brain searched frantically for an explanation. Instead, it landed on a memory I hadn't recalled in more than a decade...

The scene was from Grammie in her 80s. She had been living in a retirement home for several years, and every Thursday morning I would join her for breakfast—a visit I rarely enjoyed.

After Grampy died, Grammie had become more unpleasant with each passing year, and her general negativity could suck the life out of anyone. So, each week I spent the 20-minute drive to her residence preparing a story or a list of leading questions—anything to try keeping the conversation light and positive.

On this particular morning, however, my task was easy. A few days earlier, on a long and solitary business trip, I'd listened (for the first time) to most of Shakespeare's play *Julius Caesar*. Surprised at how many famous quotes the play contained, I was ready to share a few with Grammie to see if she recognized any.

I began by asking if she remembered, "The fault, dear Brutus, is not in our stars, but in ourselves..."

"Of course," Grammie immediately responded.

It was such a quick reaction that I couldn't help but wonder if she was bluffing and decided to test her with another quote.

"Friends, Romans, and Countrymen," I began, then (cleverly, I thought for just an instant) let the unfinished sentence hang to see if Grammie could finish that famous line.

"You're kidding!" she exclaimed. "Surely, you know Marc Antony's funeral speech?" And without pause or hesitation, she jumped in,

> … lend me your ears;
> I come to bury Caesar, not to praise him.
> The evil that men do lives after them;
> The good is oft interred with their bones;
> So let it be with Caesar. The noble Brutus
> Hath told you Caesar was ambitious:
> If it were so, it was a grievous fault,
> And grievously hath Caesar answered it.
> Here, under leave of Brutus and the rest—
> For Brutus is an honorable man;
> So are they all, all honorable men–
> Come I to speak in Caesar's funeral.

Marc Antony's oration actually continues for another 23 lines, and that morning, so did Grammie. She finished the *entire* funeral speech from memory. I was dumbfounded.

Interestingly, as that flash of memory subsided and I mentally returned to the Nevada Falls picture in front of me, "dumbfounded" was exactly the state of mind I was experiencing with my sister. With Kitty still gloating over our grandmother's trekking accomplishment, it didn't seem necessary to mention my funeral speech memory, but neither did I continue to defend my position. The combination of

Nevada Falls and Marc Antony forced me to step back. Despite the truth of my experience, there was more to Grammie than I knew.

*   *   *   *

Way back in 1978, at age 26, I had a wife, a brand-new infant daughter, a mortgage, and a social life that only rarely included my parents. For my time and place it was a fairly normal existence, and that entire year would likely have slipped into lost memory if it hadn't been for an unexpected Saturday evening, when I lay dying in the hospital emergency room.

At least I was pretty sure I was dying, because what had earlier begun as a bad stomach ache had by now risen to a level of such staggering discomfort that I was certain somebody was trying to remove part of my lower intestines with a pair of pliers.

Mercifully, the ER nurse had finally given me the biggest injection of Demerol in her arsenal, and I was drifting in and out of consciousness as a succession of doctors, nurses, and X-ray technicians poked and prodded every part of my being trying to arrive at a diagnosis. (Or maybe they were harvesting a kidney. I'm still not entirely sure.)[53] But within the haze of that long night, I remember one portion with crystal clarity.

I'd likely been in the ER for a couple of hours when, from my position on a gurney, I looked up and, after several attempts at focusing both

---

53 The doctors would eventually conclude that I had an inflamed appendix and made plans to remove it the next morning. However, as soon as that mystery organ realized its existence was in jeopardy it quickly got better. The next morning I felt fine and, with my appendix still attached, was released from the hospital.

visually and mentally, finally realized that my parents were standing over me. I was completely startled. I certainly hadn't told them about going to the hospital and, besides, I was rather confident I could take care of myself—I'd been doing it since I was 17. In my still Demerol-filled mind their presence just didn't make any sense.

"What are *you* doing here?" I finally asked.

Given the situation, it seemed a reasonable and obvious question. Apparently, Mom felt otherwise. Collecting herself, she looked down at me with a disappointed expression that, so help me, can only properly be described as *"my son has shit-for-brains."*

"Mike," she observed in obvious exasperation, "you're in the hospital! Where else would we be?"

Despite the drugs and the circumstances, I instantly recognized that voice. I'd seen that look before. Mom was in full teaching mode and my mind immediately leapt back to childhood, because, just like the broken glass episode and my failure to resolve the "Paradox of the Pronouns," I wasn't having any luck figuring out this lesson either. It would be years later (well into my own fatherhood) before I was fully able to understand Mom's "Where else would we be?" statement.

Almost all parents share a singular vision when it comes to their children: they *must* survive. It's an instinct especially strong in mothers and will generally turn even the most rational of them into female grizzly bears the moment they sense one of their young is being threatened.

So it was with Mom. At a level I couldn't yet appreciate and one more powerful than I suspect my male brain can ever fully grasp, Mom would forever experience our relationship far, far differently than I did.

Who's to say which version tells the greater truth?

*   *   *   *

Wally was Dad's best friend from high school. They joined the Navy together; they worked at the original Miner's Hardware in Culver City together. He was the best man at Mom and Dad's wedding, and in 1958, when Dad and Glenn were finally able to hire their first employee at the new Miner's Hardware in Grover Beach, Wally answered the call. He played a special role in the family and the business ever since—not the least of which was longevity.

In its long history, Miner's Hardware has been blessed with any number of employees who've worked over 10 years, a surprisingly large and faithful group who've exceeded 20 years, and a devoted handful whose service surpasses 30 years, but Wally stands alone—he worked at the Grover Beach location for 64 years.[54]

With his unique perspective on Dad, combined with his nearly lifelong family connection, Wally was the obvious choice for a different perspective on Lee Miner, and somewhere in the early 2000s we met for lunch to discuss his old friend.

It remains the single weirdest meeting I've ever attended.

This was partly due to the subject matter—my long-deceased father—and partly because, sitting there across the table from Wally, it suddenly occurred to me we were something of a cliché: two old men talking about old times. But it was mostly weird because of all the flashbacks. With each old story told, my vision blurred as younger

---

54   Wally finally retired in 2022 and died the following year at age 96.

versions of ourselves kept replacing the actual faces at the table. It was disorienting in the beginning and destined to get much worse.

We began the conversation with our own shared experiences, starting with Wally's arrival in Grover Beach, when I was 6 years old, and he was in his early 30s with a wife and two little girls (a third would follow). Miner's Hardware was in its infancy, the future uncertain, and long hours of hard work made the years race by.

We quickly relived his 40s, when I first worked in the hardware store as a high school student, then moved on to Wally's mid-50s, when I returned to the family business and began to move Miner's Hardware in new directions. Finally, we turned our attention to Dad.

I explained that I had no real knowledge or insight into Dad as a very young man up to about age 35 and was keen to hear Wally's version of that period. What followed was astonishing. It was as though I had finally asked the question Wally had been waiting his whole life to answer. He smiled, looked up and away with a Cheshire Cat kind of smile—as though he was remembering an inside joke. He paused and paused again, mentally retrieving memory after memory of a long-ago period that had obviously remained very special to him.

Finally, after putting all those remembered bits and pieces together, Wally launched into a cascade of stories featuring Dad and himself when they were both young men eager to succeed. It was a picture that was nearly 50 years old, but even after all that time it became immediately apparent that Wally still admired his old friend.

There were stories of various business deals and partnerships, of hunting and fishing trips, of parties and pranks, and altogether a feeling of shared purpose and bright futures.[55] In terms of filling in the blanks from a period I knew little about, Wally's stories were more than I could have hoped for, and, frankly, more than I could readily believe. His version of Dad didn't match up with anything I had seen or even been able to imagine.

I'm not sure how long I sat there or how incredulous my expression had become, but eventually, and likely with a tone of voice far more suspicious than intended, I replied, "Wally, are you telling me that as a young man my father was the kind of guy who was admired by men and adored by women?"

Wally paused thoughtfully, considered the question, considered again the source and the 50-plus years of shared history between us, then, and without a hint of rancor in his voice, replied calmly (and for added effect, slowly), "Well, he was sure a hell of a lot better at that age than you were!"

A very long pause followed this last comment as I struggled to reconcile Wally's unexpected observation against my own internal narrative (which didn't particularly appreciate comparisons between my father and me). I was fine with Wally throwing Dad a bone, but to suggest outright superiority was a little much.

Nevertheless, the more I considered Wally's singular knowledge of the two people in question, and the more I thought back to my own journey through those years, the less sure I became of my assumed preeminence. Casting aside any false modesty, I could justifiably lay claim to a handful of impressive talents during my late 20s and early

---

55 It was Wally who provided the ambulance story (Chapter 14) and added detail to the pogo stick incident (Chapter 15).

30s but, truth be told, I probably had two handfuls of remarkable faults. In short, the combination of my early strengths and weaknesses hadn't set the bar all that high, and Wally's unexpected accusation might well have been right.

Honestly, the longer I sat there looking across the table at Wally, and the more I reconsidered the intersection of the three lives being discussed, the more curiously funny our entire conversation became. Indeed, as a few of my more notable screw-ups from that long-ignored period flashed before my mind's eye, the funnier Wally's comment felt, until, finally, I was laughing so hard that most of the remaining patrons in the restaurant had turned in our direction hoping to share in the joke.

Wally had been part of my life for as long as I'd been alive, and, until just before my 29th birthday, so had Dad (who died in 1981). For the three of us, then, our respective experiences and memories, our successes and failures—everything that made up who we were—had flowed around, between, past, and through one another on so many levels, and from so many directions, and through such different lenses, that it suddenly seemed foolish to assume any single view could be both accurate and sufficient. Like standing on three different continents to watch the sunset, we all saw something different.

CHAPTER 44

Bee and the Family Business[56]

Whe n Abe died back in late 1974, Bee (who was then 68 years old) quickly found herself in a forced re-evaluation of her life's direction. Before her lay a myriad of choices. Her skills—in business and with people—were exceptional; her health was robust, her finances significant. She could have traveled the world or indulged in a new hobby. She could have seriously considered one of the many suitors who began to appear or joined any number of social groups.

Perhaps she considered all these and more, but she soon chose going back to work. Leisure time, she believed, could only be enjoyed in moderation—too much wasn't just decadent, it was dumb.

---

56 For the chronologically curious or confused: Miner's Hardware in Grover Beach was opened in 1956 by Lee and Glenn. Wally arrived in 1958. Lee sold his share of the business in 1966. Bee began working part-time at Miner's Hardware in 1975, and I began my 43-year career in 1979. Susie worked part-time in the 1980s and mostly full-time from 1995-2005, Amy and Bethany started working at the stores in the early 1990s (when they were in middle school), my cousin Kim started her 23-year career in the family business in 1995, and Paul Filice (Amy's husband) started his career in 2005. Finally, Giacomo, Lena, and Celia (fifth generation) began working in the mid-2010s.

"If you have cake every day," she liked to explain, "pretty soon it won't taste very good."

So, in early 1975, just a few months after becoming a widow, Bee returned to her roots—or at least one of her roots—when she took a part-time job at Miner's Hardware, working Monday through Friday from 9 to 1. It was a job she would keep for the next 22 years, and one that would see her engage with family, employees, and the world in general in ways she never had before.

Back then Miner's Hardware was a small operation, and Bee, like all employees, worked in every department. Later, as the business grew and tasks became more compartmentalized, she turned her attention towards fasteners (nuts, bolts, screws, and the like).

Fasteners, by the way, remain one of the stores' larger departments—there are hundreds of bins, shelves, boxes, and drawers, containing thousands of different fasteners, all of which have different diameters, threads, lengths, strengths, and coatings. As departments go, none are more difficult. The inventory is seemingly endless, and the differences in the products are often subtle and crucial. (Trust me when I tell you that a left-handed nut will not work on a right-handed bolt, and, even though they look the same, a 10-24 TPI (threads per inch) bolt will not replace a 10-32 TPI bolt.

The result of all this complexity is that nearly every customer who enters the fastener department needs help, and Bee loved helping people more than just about anything else.

She also took the family business seriously and wanted to see it succeed. So, when we opened our second store in Arroyo Grande (the same year Bee turned 80), she began splitting her time between both locations—a schedule she maintained with little variation until finally retiring in 1994, at age 90.

*   *   *   *

Throughout the years Bee worked at Miner's Hardware, traveling salesmen were still common, and there were several who regularly called on us from various companies. They represented lines like power tools, paint, faucets, and so on. It was a tough job and few of them lasted more than a couple of years. Except for one: the National Hardware Salesman.

National Hardware was a U.S. manufacturer of hinges, hasps, snaps, hooks, and assorted basic hardware, and for more than 20 years they were one of our largest suppliers. Sadly, like so many U.S. manufacturers, they would eventually succumb to cheaper Chinese imports, but in the decades leading up to the turn of the century, the company was well run, their products excellent, and they treated their salesmen unusually well. In turn, their salesmen tended to stay, and for more than a dozen years the same young man arrived every three weeks to take an order.

As salesmen went, he was every bit as good as the company he worked for, and, because his products were located next to fasteners, he and Bee soon knew each other well. More than that, they were friends. Bee knew his schedule, his family, where he went on vacation, and both of them looked forward to his every-three-week visit, which always began with a short but warm conversation between them.

My relationship with him was much more utilitarian. Typically, we'd meet formally once or twice a year to discuss new products, displays, promotions, etc., and it was during one of those meetings (sometime in the early 1990s) that he unexpectedly went off-script …

"Mike," he began, "I call on over 40 stores, and your two are always the best in my territory. In fact, they're among the best in the entire country. Do you know why?"

Naturally I assumed his compliment was directed at me and expected him to answer with "management" or "leadership" and maybe throw in an "inspired" or "brilliant" for good measure.

"Your grandmother," he said emphatically.

Huh? I thought to myself. *My grandmother?*

I must have looked particularly confused at that moment, or maybe the salesman was just uncomfortable with the long pause that followed, but either way, he soon continued.

"Do you know how special she is? That she gets down on her knees every time a little kid wanders into her department, so she can make eye contact with them? Do you know that she never takes a break, and that her department is cleaner and neater than any others I visit? And, best of all, though she never asks for help, everyone else in that department is working doubly hard because they don't want her to be disappointed."

It's right about here that I'd like to share the thoughtful and magnanimous response I gave to the salesman's compliment, but, truthfully, I'm not sure I responded at all. Instead, I distinctly remember wondering if, next, he was going to tell me the sky was blue or make some other equally obvious pronouncement.

Of course, I knew Bee did those things and had that effect on others—she was always like that. She'd been greeting little kids eyeball-to-eyeball since, well, since I was a little kid (and presumably before that). And in terms of her work ethic, of course she didn't ask for help, or take a break. She was *working*.

When she was a child, working had meant survival for Bee and her family. In her many business ventures with Abe, it was the difference between success or failure. Now, in her 80s and working to help the family hardware store succeed, she found purpose, accomplishment, and the opportunity to give to others.

In short, Bee enjoyed working, and whether she was helping customers, or doing household chores, or tending to her garden and fruit trees, she worked every single day. It was a practice she maintained right up until the end, and not even a broken bone could change that routine…

*   *   *   *

Throughout her life, Bee was a voracious reader and, especially as she got older, could often be found in the late afternoon sitting in her favorite chair and enjoying whatever book was at hand.[57]

It was just this situation—Bee in her late 80s, sitting comfortably in her living room on a Friday afternoon and enjoying a good book—when the doorbell rang.

---

[57] Bee mostly read popular novels but was always ready to try something new. During Abe's long illness, for example, I lent her my copy of *The Hobbit*. She loved it, and when I mentioned that Tolkien had also written the three-volume *Lord of the Rings,* she borrowed those next and read them all.

Bethany, Bee, and Amy Miner at Miner's Hardware in Grover Beach, 1994.

Apparently, she'd been sitting too long with her legs crossed and hadn't realized one of them had fallen asleep. So, when she jumped up to get the door, the leg gave way, causing her to fall and break her left foot.

Fortunately, it was a simple fracture. She was fitted with a walking cast and instructed to rest for at least a week. Inconsistently, however, the doctor also mentioned that she could walk as much as her pain would allow. Naturally, to Bee, this meant she could return to work on Monday.

This seemed a particularly bad idea to me, and upon arriving for breakfast that Monday morning I was firm in my recommendation that she take the rest of the week off.

Bee wasn't listening.

In fact, the only concession I was able to extract from her was a promise to let me pick her up at 9 a.m. That way she wouldn't have to use her broken left foot to push the clutch on the old manual-shift car she still drove. Nothing went as planned after that …

At work, the typical Monday morning disorder awaited me and, despite my best efforts, it was already a little after 9 by the time I got to the fasteners department to begin planning how best to handle Bee's return to work. After a quick reconnoiter I found a small stool, which I carried over to the department manager to better explain my plan.

"When I return with Bee," I began, "I'd like you to start moving boxes from the fastener order on the dock to the aisle she'll be working in. That way Bee can still put the order away and sit on the stool as necessary."

At this, the department manager, whose eyes hadn't moved from the stool I'd just placed in the aisle, finally looked up and, with an expression that was both pained and confused, pleaded for mercy. "But Mike," he exclaimed, "she's your *grandmother*. Why are you making her come back to work so soon?"

"What?" I heard myself cry out. But it was too late. Before I could explain my innocence, we both saw Bee limping down the aisle in our direction. Clearly disappointed in my lack of punctuality, she'd left home at 9:01 and driven to work—broken foot, manual clutch, and all.

*   *   *   *

There was another benefit of working, which Bee used with remarkable effect—the opportunity to leverage work connections into social connections. Once, for example, when I unexpectedly stopped by her house over the weekend, I was surprised to find Bee at her kitchen table enjoying lunch with a fellow employee and his wife. (Something I later learned she did with regularity.) But, my favorite story about Bee's ability to expand her world by reaching out to others was given to me years after she was gone.

Throughout her workweek, Bee typically left the hardware store shortly after 1 p.m. and headed out for lunch. Still dressed in her red smock (the hardware store's uniform), she would choose one of several nearby restaurants and eat lunch alone. It was a routine that soon became well-known by all the various staffs and one that made a special impression on a young restaurant owner—an entrepreneur not unlike Abe, who would soon be on his way to more interesting and profitable endeavors.[58]

Decades later, and a few years after Bee died, our paths happened to cross at a business symposium in which he was one of the speakers and I was one of the hosts. Although we'd never met, each of us slightly knew the other by reputation, and at the conclusion of the event he approached me with a most unexpected question.

"Are you related to Bee Miner?" he asked hopefully.

Smiling, I explained she was my grandmother.

"A long time ago," he began with his own broad smile, "I knew your grandmother well. She was a regular customer at the restaurant, and always came in after the lunchtime rush."

---

58 He would become rather famous for selling square, clear suckers flavored with tequila in which (unbelievably but true) a worm larva was placed in the middle. Apparently, the larva are actually edible (if one's into that sort of thing) and customers around the world gobbled them up, literally.

He paused for a moment, as though setting the scene carefully in his mind before continuing.

"It was a visit I soon looked forward to, and whenever time allowed, I'd sit at her table. Sometimes we'd talk about work or about life in general—I even remember a few stories about her growing up on a farm—but, whatever the subject, it was always a delight to be with her."

Pausing a second time, his expression changed again. The smile was still there, but it was more wistful than before. Perhaps he was remembering a favorite story Bee had shared, or a special conversation between the two of them, but whatever it was, his visits with Bee had clearly been important to him.

Finally, he said, "I just wanted you to know how much I enjoyed her company, and how sorry I am she's gone."

I knew just how he felt …

CHAPTER 45

Nearing the End

As the 20th century drew to an end so too did my three remaining ancestors—Mom, Grammie Peggie, and Bee. Mom died from cirrhosis in 1996, and the next year Grammie Peggie began moving into a series of assisted living facilities that offered ever increasing levels of care.

Ornery to the end, Grammie Peggie was never featured as "Resident of the Month" at any of the places she lived. However, she always had a smile for me each time I arrived for our Thursday morning visit, and to my great surprise I found myself genuinely missing her abrasive company after she died in the spring of 2000.

Bee (of course) navigated this last portion of her life differently. Physically she was still remarkably healthy at age 90 (in 1994), but her short-term memory was failing. Knowing it was time, she retired from the hardware store and gave up driving.

Those two changes alone were monumentally disruptive and her ongoing struggle to adapt was destined to get more difficult with each passing year. Yet, with the eventual help of a part-time caregiver, Bee was able to live independently right up until the end.

The girls and I (and others) continued to visit as before, but conversations gradually became limited to events from the past, and eventually even those memories began to dim.

It was a heartbreaking process to watch, and much more sinister than one might realize. Without being able to lay down new memories, a simple problem that was resolved 20 minutes ago will cycle back as a new problem, and conversations that require any back-and-forth become impossible. Even reading a book became impractical, because the characters and plot line keep disappearing.

Worst of all—and most cruelly so—Bee sometimes knew it was happening. As haunting as those moments she once described of turning to say something to Abe, then realizing he was gone, Bee regularly experienced fleeting periods (a minute or so) of startling clarity. Those were moments of anguish, and on the few times I was present it was like watching a third-person narrative come to life—as though she was looking at herself in a mirror, realizing that her mind was dying and leaving her body behind. It was hard not to despair at the senselessness of it.

Yet she never gave in. Much like being caught in a maze, when one doorway of her mind became stuck or closed off forever, Bee would wander down a different path looking for another opening.

Gardening worked. An orange will tell you when it's ripe, a tomato plant when it needs water, and for a long time Bee was still sending all of us home with seasonal fresh fruit, avocados, and vegetables.

Unexpectedly, golf tournaments on TV worked, and Bee became a regular fan. At first her newfound love of the game was a great mystery. She had never before been interested in any sport. However, upon once sitting down to watch along with her, I immediately realized what an advantage (necessity, really) a failing short-term memory provided: there has to be some way to forget how mind-numbingly boring the game really is.

Likely there are legions of golf fans (perhaps unaware they have memory issues) who will disagree with my assessment, but watching Bee find enjoyment in those televised golf tournaments reminded me exactly of watching a fishbowl—bright, colorful, and completely fascinating for about three minutes—the very attributes that fit Bee's condition, and she soon became the owner of a new 40-gallon saltwater aquarium.

Over the next few years that aquarium become inseparably linked with Bee, and together that combination brought more joy, more insights, and more stories than anyone could have imagined …

CHAPTER 46

The Aquarium

It turns out that maintaining a 40-gallon saltwater aquarium is not as easy as one might imagine. If the water gets too hot or too cold, the fish die. If the salt ratio or PH ratio moves beyond a narrow band, the fish die. Too much food or too little food—the fish die. Sometimes they died just out of spite.

But all those lethal problems were unknown when I arrived at Bee's house one Saturday morning with a giant box, lots of little boxes, and a long list of instructions. We settled on placing the aquarium on a waist-high counter that separated the kitchen from the kitchen table—a perfect location that allowed viewing from both rooms—and, after a few hours of installing the pump, heater, filter, salt, distilled water, gravel, rocks, and more, the aquarium stood ready, and by this, I mean it was ready to dispatch any life form I introduced.

Fish, hermit crabs, sea snails—they all perished in "The Tank of Death," and for that first week I was well on my way to becoming the aquarium store's best customer of the year. By week two, however, something started to work. The ratios all came into alignment, the water cleared up, and new replacement fish were living for days on end.

It was a great success and Bee soon knew (and loved) every critter in there. For the ones that liked to hide, she knew their secret places. For the ones that were always hungry, she fed them first; and for the timid and slow, she made sure they got their share later. She cared about them all.

Not that this was unusual. With the possible exception of scorpions (from her years in the Mojave Desert), Bee cared for just about everything that lived … and therein lay my first problem, because Bee's life-is-sacred mentality was rather at odds with how the aquarium actually functioned.

About a month or two after things settled down, and we'd all begun to think the six resident fish would live long and happy lives, they didn't. I arrived one morning expecting breakfast as usual, only to find Bee distressfully pointing to one of the fish. It was floating upside down at the top of the tank—dead as a doornail. Knowing that its decomposing body was slowly poisoning the entire tank, I quickly scooped it up with a net, tossed it in the garbage disposal, and turned on the switch.

Poor Bee. While I still doubt she was expecting a formal burial in the backyard (complete with flowers and a reading), her shocked expression made it obvious she had imagined something a bit more thoughtful than the garbage disposal.

I had flunked the Fish Compassion Test.

Frankly, I never could pass that test. Try as I might, my feelings for the fish were never able to rise much above the feelings I had for the plants in my front yard: if they died, I had a problem. Clearly, this wasn't the level of caring Bee was expecting. Yet, just as clearly, I was going to be tested with more dead fish in the future. I needed a workaround.

So, the next time I found a fish floating upside down (and there were many next times), I gently scooped it up, placed it in a plastic bag filled with water and explained to Bee that, because the fish was very sick, I would take it to the aquarium store, where they would treat it with special medicine.

It was miraculous. Each time I handed the aquarium store a dead fish floating in a plastic bag, they gave it a dose of my credit card and in minutes I left with a brand-new healthy fish (exactly the same size and color). This would then be returned to Bee's aquarium, with the good news that the special medicine had worked.

It was an elegant solution. Bee was pleasantly relieved every time a fish was "saved," and every time she stayed glued to the aquarium, watching to make sure it stayed that way.

*   *   *   *

The aquarium contained a typical assortment of colorful saltwater fish: angelfish, clownfish, damselfish, and Bee's favorite, the puffer fish. Actually, the puffer fish was everybody's favorite. It was slow, ungainly, and so ridiculously ugly that you couldn't help but feel sorry for the thing.

An obvious example of natural selection run amok, the puffer fish was shaped more or less like an ice cube—about 1 inch on each side, with a disproportionally large tail sticking out the back. On its square face were two big eyes set far apart, with a prominent nose in the middle and largish mouth just below that. The rest of its body was smooth and flat except for two tiny fins—one on either side—which were its only means of propulsion. The big tail on the back was only used as a rudder.

Yet, as odd as it looked on the outside, its personality was stranger still. All the other fish fell into two distinct groups: nervous and narcissistic. The former spent their days anxiously darting between hiding places, while the latter, eager to show off their regal good looks, were constantly on parade.

The puffer fish followed a different path. As though practicing mindfulness, it would wander slowly about every part of the aquarium, seemingly amazed at the miracle of existence and grateful for each day (which may well have been the case, considering where it lived). It was especially interested in Bee, and whenever she got up close, the puffer fish would typically swim right up to the glass and get nose-to-nose with her.

It was charming behavior for any creature, especially so for a fish, and each time I'd arrive for breakfast, Bee was sure to tell me about the puffer fish's latest antics. Of course, with her worsening short-term memory problems, each new report was pretty much the same as her last report, and this growing tendency to repeat fish stories was what eventually got me into trouble with the girls.

By now the girls were both in college and their visits to Grammie Bee's had become increasingly irregular. Typically, they visited on their own when they could, but on this particular morning, in a rare confluence of schedules, we'd all managed to arrive for breakfast at the same time.

It was a mini reunion, and while Bee (who was now in her mid-90s) had trouble following any new conversation, she was, as always, thrilled to listen to her great-granddaughters' adventures. She was also ready to tell a story in return, and this lively exchange soon turned to the aquarium as Bee began to describe the activities of the puffer fish.

We'd all heard this report before, but to the girls' and my mutual surprise, Bee finished this version with a first-ever demonstration of the puffer fish's ungainly movements. Standing up from her chair, she began by flapping her hands by her side to show us how its little fins worked. For the rudder motion of its tail, Bee needed more room, and after pushing her chair to one side, she bent about halfway to perpendicular at the waist, then, with her butt sticking out in back, quickly swooshed it to one side.

It was a hysterically funny pantomime, and the girls and I doubled over in laughter. Watching her audience, Bee, who wasn't entirely sure she got the joke, was nevertheless so pleased with the merriment around her table that she nearly took a bow.

With the show over, we settled down to breakfast and more conversation until it was time to leave. Taking a last look at the aquarium, the girls and I lined up to give Bee a hug and kiss goodbye, when (I must confess) the 12-year-old-boy part of my brain—knowing Bee would have forgotten her earlier performance—suddenly interrupted and asked, "So, how does the puffer fish move around?"

Bee seemed delighted at the question and immediately gave us all another performance of flapping hands and swooshing tail that I thought was even funnier than the first one. The girls, I'm afraid, were not nearly as amused, and, though a few laughs leaked out, they were still throwing dagger looks in my direction warning me not to do it again.

I didn't, but even as I feigned contrition in front of my daughters, I knew that had Bee been able to get the joke, she would have laughed right along with me.

Something of a prankster herself (once serving pancakes with a circular piece of bedsheet baked into the middle, making them uncut-able), Bee had always been self-deprecating—keenly aware that if there actually was a center to the universe, she didn't live near it.

It was a quality I would need to remember later …

A few Christmases after Bee's passing, most of the family was gathered around the table for dinner when the conversation turned to members no longer present. A small assortment of stories had been passed around when the girls began remembering the aquarium. Taking turns, they soon arrived at Bee's now famous puffer fish performance, when they suddenly stopped and Amy said, "Dad, you should tell the rest."

"Yeah," Bethany chimed in, "you tell this better than we do."

Never shy about responding to such a request, I immediately launched into the complete story and, with the audience's growing enthusiasm, soon found myself standing up from my chair to demonstrate Bee's gestures. It was a hell of a performance and, just as I finished with a swoosh, I looked up to see the girls both giggling at one another across the table. I'd been had.

The whole table was laughing (at me) and soon so was I. Bee would have loved every part of it.

*   *   *   *

For the aquarium's first couple of years, Bee was able to feed the fish by herself. Every morning she'd look in the freezer to find cubes of premixed frozen fish food—each individually marked with the day of the week and ready to drop into the tank. She made a few mistakes, but for a good long while the fish survived the occasional missed day or double feeding. In fact, the only serious problem during that period was caused by someone else.

It was a typical Monday morning at Grammie Bee's. We'd shared breakfast, I'd listened to a few old stories and the latest fish report, but when Bee went to feed the fish, we both realized it was the last cube of fish food she had in her freezer.

"No problem," I told her as I was leaving. "I'll drop off more fish food in the morning."

Apparently, Bee latched on to "morning," which as far as she was concerned meant sometime before 7 a.m. For me "morning" meant after the aquarium store opened at 9:00 a.m., and my plan was to arrive at Bee's house with the fish food shortly afterwards.

Neither happened. At work that Tuesday morning, one problem after another demanded my immediate attention. So, after waiting for hours, Bee called at 9:30 a.m. to check on my whereabouts. I apologized for my tardiness, tried to reassure her that the fish would be fine, and said that I'd arrive in half an hour.

That didn't happen either. Just after 10 a.m., Bee called again. Our conversation bounced between my continuing apologies for being late and Bee's growing concern that the fish were near death. Finally, in a last attempt to convey the seriousness of the situation, she gravely explained, "The fish were doing *a lot* of swimming."

I'm afraid it was nearly 11:00 a.m. that morning when I finally walked through Bee's front door with the cheerful news that I had the life-saving fish food in hand.

No response. I walked into the kitchen and there, standing silently next to the aquarium and looking intently at its contents, was Bee. I froze mid-step. Hundreds, maybe thousands, of little bits of something were floating throughout the tank.

For an instant I wondered if Bee's earlier warnings might actually have been correct. Were those little bits of shredded fish? Had they attacked one another in some hunger-crazed feeding frenzy?

No. Looking through the muck, I soon spotted a fish, then another, and another, until I'd found all six. Whatever the mystery bits were, they weren't fish.

Grabbing a net, I scooped up a large sample of bits, inspected them carefully, squished some together, and groaned at the obvious conclusion. Yet, even as I knew the answer, I wanted badly to be wrong. "Bee," I asked hopefully, "*please* tell me you didn't feed the fish a scrambled egg."

Already starting to forget the sequence of events, Bee nervously examined the bits of something in my hand, then followed my gaze to the frying pan still sitting on the stove. We both knew the answer.

"Well," she offered. "They were *really* hungry."

"*What?*" I heard someone cry out.

It was the Time-Management portion of my brain panicking at the sudden realization that cleaning up this mess was going to take hours out of the day's carefully planned schedule. Yet, even as Mr. Time-Management continued whining about urgent phone calls, and meetings, and reports, the rest of my mind turned towards Bee.

Clearly upset, Bee understood she'd made a mistake and wanted badly to fix it. She just didn't know how. She wasn't even sure what the mistake was anymore.

For a long moment I just stood there—looking slowly back and forth between Bee and the aquarium. Then, in a mental exchange so vivid it felt like I was watching a movie, I saw the rest of my mind rise up in unison, grab Mr. Time-Management by his metaphysical neck, and give him a thrashing that was nearly fatal.

Yes, there were some urgent phone calls and meetings I was going to miss, but for my whole life Bee had been showing me that most of those would never really matter. They weren't important. Instead, people were important; family was important. Sometimes even fish were important.

The mess in the aquarium? That was just an egg …

CHAPTER 47

Epilogue

A couple of years after Dad died, Mom married Gerry Vallem. A fellow retired schoolteacher, Gerry was a good man and a good grandfather to the girls. He survived Mom by almost a decade, and throughout those last years Gerry and I remained close—frequently meeting over lunch to keep up on each other's lives and to discuss (and debate) the events of the day.

It was a relationship we both enjoyed, but not long after Gerry reached 86 (still as mentally sharp as ever), his emphysema became critical. Admitted to the hospital in severe respiratory distress, his doctor explained that the situation was serious and wondered what Gerry's wishes were if he should lapse into a coma. Specifically, the doctor needed to know if Gerry wanted to be resuscitated if he stopped breathing. Until that moment, when health and life had been assumed, Gerry had always dismissed this option. Now, for the first time, he hesitated and considered the question carefully before finally responding, "Well, I guess you could try a couple of times."

I happened to be in the ICU during this exchange and, apparently, my complete surprise at Gerry's sudden change of heart must have shown in my expression more than I intended, because he turned to me next and explained dryly, "Well, this used to be an academic question. Now, I see it's personal."

If there was nothing else about Gerry that I had liked or admired, this wonderful understatement would have endeared him to me forever, and as he laid there in his hospital bed with a smirk on his face and a smile in his eyes, we both burst out laughing at the irony and wisdom within his response.

For all the main characters in this book, life *was* personal—a one-of-a-kind encounter as unique as their genome—and within those experiences lie inspiration, warning, and an appreciation that life is short and precious.

For Mom I think about how much fun it would have been to meet her during the filming of *Mary Wanna* or how exciting to be there on her first day of class as a new teacher.

I see Dad—just a few months before he died—holding his little granddaughter with newfound joy. If he'd lived, maybe he would have risen to the occasion.

And Abe—a man so ruddy with life he all but leaps out of every memory I have of him, and Glenn, who early on believed in my ability and later helped me avoid more mistakes than I ever thought possible.

I remember Grammie—a woman who surprised me more times than I've recounted.

And Grampy, who reappears every time I hug one of my grandchildren and the joys of childhood come rushing back.

Finally, there is Bee, and I smile for every breakfast we ever shared.

In truth, they were all bigger and bolder than I'm able to describe, and probably more ordinary than I'm willing to admit. In truth, I'm not sure they mattered in the grand scheme of the universe, but I can tell you *they mattered to me.*

I remember them all, and I am grateful.

Final Note:

At the end of 2022 Miner's Hardware passed to the fourth generation: Amy, (her husband) Paul, and Bethany. Together with the fifth generation—Giacomo, Lena, and Celia—they are all busily engaged in making their own stories.

Bibliography

South Dakota Historical Society. Drawn to the Land.
(https://history.sd.gov/museum/docs/HomesteadingDakota.pdf)

General Patton's World War II Training Ground in the Mojave
(https://www.nps.gov/articles/pattonmojave.htm)

The Spruce Goose
(https://www.evergreenmuseum.org/exhibit/the-spruce-goose/)

The Great White Fleet
(https://www.history.navy.mil/research/histories/ship-histories/the-great-white-fleet.html)

William Mulholland
(https://www.watereducation.org/aquapedia/william-mulholland)
(https://en.wikipedia.org/wiki/William_Mulholland)

Theadore Roosevelt
(https://www.whitehouse.gov/about-the-white-house/presidents/theodore-roosevelt/)
(https://en.wikipedia.org/wiki/Theodore_Roosevelt)

Operation Torch
(https://en.wikipedia.org/wiki/Operation_Torch#:~:text=Torch%20was%20a%20compromise%20operation,Italy%20on%20a%20limited%20scale)
(https://en.wikipedia.org/wiki/Operation_Torch#:~:text=Torch%20was%20a%20compromise%20operation,Italy%20on%20a%20limited%20scale)

Voyager Spacecraft
(https://science.nasa.gov/mission/voyager/)
(https://en.wikipedia.org/wiki/Voyager_program)

Information Age
(https://en.wikipedia.org/wiki/Information_Age)

Edward T. O'Donnell, *America in the Gilded Age and Progressive Era,* The Teaching Company

Roosevelt, Theadore. *The Naval War of 1812,* The Easton Press, 2011

McNamara, Robert. *In Retrospect: The Tragedy and Lessons of Vietnam,* Random House, 1995

Woodger, David F., Burg, Elin. *The 1980's,* Eyewitness, 2006

Gilbert, Martin. *A History of the 20th Century,* Harper Colins, 2002

Churchill, Winston. *The Second World War,* Folio Society, 2000

Klosterman, Chuck, *The Nineties: A Book,* Penguin Books, 2002

Halberstam, David. *The Fifties,* Open Road Media, 1995